WORLD

R Any oad,

C Any ost

**The Cambodia and
Congo Conflicts—
Real-life Accounts of
Peace in Crisis**

LISA M. ROHRICK

Christian Publications
CAMP HILL, PENNSYLVANIA

Any Road, Any Cost

Christian Publications, Inc.
3825 Hartzdale Drive, Camp Hill, PA 17011
www.cpi-horizon.com

Faithful, biblical publishing since 1883

ISBN: 0-87509-798-7
© 1998 by Christian Publications, Inc.

Contents

Preface

It was Thursday, July 24, 1997, and I was at Mahaffey Camp of The Christian and Missionary Alliance in Western Pennsylvania. One of the speakers that morning was Joyce McCabe, missionary to Congo, Africa.

Joyce and her husband Kevin, along with their three children, had arrived in the U.S. only three days earlier, after being evacuated from Congo's civil war. She told of bullets aimed at their small plane as they left the Brazzaville airport. And she told of receiving an encouraging e-mail note from their son when they were safely across the river in the neighboring country. He wrote, "Remember, God is good—all the time."

Following the meeting, I strolled across the campgrounds with my friend and colleague Marilynne Foster.

"You know, I think that's a story that should be written," she said.

We talked for a few minutes of how one could approach such a project before Marilynne concluded, "And you're the one to write it!"

At the next meeting of the Christian Publications editorial board, the idea was presented and approved. You hold in your hands the results of that decision.

I wish to express my thanks to the missionary teams from Congo and Cambodia. Thank you all for being willing to tell me your stories—in person, over the phone and by e-mail—and for working with me to get it straight. Without your willing cooperation, this book would not have happened. Thanks also to Ron and Myra Brown, Jay and Bev Bellamy, Carol Erbst, Tina Gilstrap and Kevin and Joyce McCabe for supplying the Congo photographs and to Mike Roark for the Cambodia ones.

Marilynne, thanks for getting me into this, for your suggestions along the way and for seeing it through to the end. Thanks for your skillful editing and for pushing me to do my best, not allowing me to settle for "good enough."

Also thanks to my friends and colleagues in CPI's editorial department for hitting the "fast-forward button" and still calling me your friend in spite of the crazy schedule to get this book through the typesetting and proofreading process.

And thanks to those of you who give to the Great Commission Fund and the Global Advance Fund of The Christian and Missionary Alliance. It's your gifts that enable people like those you'll read about in these pages to do their jobs—proclaiming the good news of Jesus Christ.

Lisa M. Rohrick
Alliance Missionary Appointee

Any Road, Any Cost

Leaving the safe and familiar
With their hearts set on a heavenly prize
There were some who laid down their nets
And some who laid down their lives
Not sure where they were going
But they did not have to know
'Cause they knew who had called them
And they said, "We will go"

Down any road at any cost
Wherever You lead we will follow
Because we know that You've called us
To take up our cross
Down any road at any cost

It may be fear that we're feeling
When we see what we must sacrifice
But You promised You'll go with us
So we'll trust with our lives
It's Your love that compels us
To do what You've called us to do
And be completely abandoned to You

Down any road at any cost . . .

by Scott Krippayne and Tony Wood
1996 BMG Songs, Inc., Gospel Division
Used by permission.

Introduction

The road was blocked. The convoy had no choice but to stop. Twenty or more armed and angry men surrounded the vehicles, some in uniform, others in civilian clothes. Many had a gun in one hand and a beer bottle in the other. One look into the reddened eyes of their leader confirmed that these men were not in control of their actions.

Their wild eyes darted back and forth as the soldiers yelled unintelligible threats at the top of their lungs. With menacing looks they pointed their guns at the windows, seemingly unbothered by the fact that many of the faces staring out at them belonged to wide-eyed children ranging in age from two to sixteen.

Some of the forty-one Americans and Canadians in the convoy's four vehicles were panicking, crying and shouting hysterical commands to the drivers, as if their obedience could somehow change the predicament. Others sat calmly—some praying, some reassuring their children, others lost in thought, wondering what their fate would be.

Why are they stopping us? What do they want with us?

The group, twenty-three of whom were Christian and Missionary Alliance missionaries and their children, was at the entrance to the airport in Brazzaville, Congo in Central Africa. It was June 7, 1997. Two days of severe fighting had led the North Americans to decide that evacuation from the crippled city was the wisest thing. Two small planes were waiting to make as many trips as necessary to shuttle the group out of the country. If only these frenzied men would move their roadblock and let the convoy through!

Is this where we're going to die? Joyce McCabe wondered, looking at her frightened eleven-year-old daughter, Shealyn.

* * *

Just one month later, on the other side of the globe, a similar scene unfolded. On July 10, 1997, after a weekend of falling rockets and flying mortars, the team of Alliance missionaries in Phnom Penh, Cambodia joined hundreds of others fleeing the shaken city.

Things were quiet in Phnom Penh that day. But tensions ran high. Rumors were rife that the silence was temporary—merely a brief intermission after the nerve-wracking opening scene of civil war.

A tearful group of missionaries made their

way down devastated streets toward Pochentong International Airport at the city's edge.
Driving past looted gas stations and factories
and burned-out homes, they felt guilty that
they could flee while their Cambodian friends
didn't have that option.

Blooming flame trees lined the road with bril-
liant color. Towering coconut palms stood behind them, waving their vivid green fronds in
the early afternoon breeze. But the missionaries, each lost in troubled thought, didn't notice
their beauty.

Moments later they stood at the entrance to
the airport and sadly watched one of their
Cambodian colleagues climb back into the
Mission truck and drive away.

Will we ever see him again? they wondered,
joining the mingling crowd of evacuees waiting
to board outgoing planes. *Will we ever see this
city again?*

Part 1

The Congo Road

"And the peace of God,
which transcends all understanding,
will guard your hearts
and your minds
in Christ Jesus."

(Philippians 4:7)

Map of Africa

highlighting the area in which the story takes place

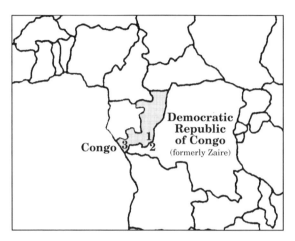

1. Brazzaville
2. Kinshasa
3. Pointe Noire

Map of Brazzaville, Congo

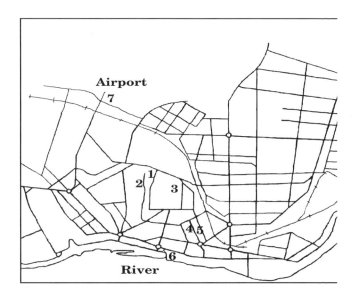

1. Brazzaville Center for Christian Studies
2. McCabe residence
3. Bellamy residence
4. Brown/Noel (Hotalen) duplex
5. Erbst residence
6. The U.S. Embassy
7. Intersection at which the convoy of North
   Americans was stopped on the way to the air

The Congo Team

*The Christian and Missionary Alliance
—Republic of Congo, June 1997*

Jay and Beverly Bellamy
  Benjamin (BJ) - age 7
  Daniel - age 5
  Lauren - age 2

Ronald and Myra Brown
  Bethany - age 14
  Rebecca - age 10

Nelson and Carole Cook (with
International Fellowship of Alliance Professionals)

Carolyn Erbst

Ronald Julian
  (on home assignment in the U.S.)
  Travis - age 8
  Brandon - age 5
  Leticia - age 3

Kevin and Joyce McCabe
  Shawn - age 17 (at International
    Christian Academy, Côte d'Ivoire)
  Shannon - age 14
  Shealyn - age 11

David and Tamara Noel
(on home assignment in the U.S.)
   Judson - age 9
   Katie - age 6

Ruth Sterneman
(evacuated to South Africa with malaria)

The Christian and Missionary Alliance —Democratic Republic of Congo (formerly Zaire), June 1997

Marion Dicke
(in South Africa, accompanying Ruth Sterneman)

Stan and Connie Hotalen (evacuated
from Kinshasa to Brazzaville in April 1997)
   Jeana - age 16
   Christa - age 13
   Jason - age 11
   Sean - age 5

James and Dawn Sawatsky (back in Kinshasa
after evacuation to Brazzaville in April 1997)

Anne Stephens (evacuated from Kinshasa to
Brazzaville in April 1997)

Chapter 1

"I Don't Do Sleepovers"

Thursday, June 5, 1997

The phone rang at Kevin and Joyce McCabe's home in Brazzaville, Congo.

It's probably that lady about the piano, Joyce thought as she lifted the receiver. The freshly shined and polished piano sat on the porch waiting to be picked up by its new owner. It belonged to missionary colleague Ron Julian who was home in the U.S. After Ron's wife Nancy had lost her battle with cancer a few months earlier, the McCabes had agreed to sell her piano for him. A French woman wanted to purchase it and had arranged to pick it up that morning.

But the phone call had nothing to do with the piano. It was the U.S. Embassy.

"I'm sure you have heard the shooting around the city this morning," the American voice said.

"Yes," Joyce affirmed.

"The fighting is most intense in the Mpila neighborhood. Please pass on the message that Americans should stay out of that area." Joyce knew that neighborhood was the home of presidential candidate Denis Sassou Nguesso and wondered if he was somehow involved in this latest conflict.

A few months earlier, in anticipation of civil unrest that might accompany the presidential election scheduled for July 27, 1997, the embassy set up a warden system. Embassy personnel would call a few wardens to pass on messages for American citizens. The wardens, in turn, would relay the messages to the dozen or more people on their lists. Joyce McCabe was one of the wardens.

The McCabes heard the first shots shortly after breakfast that Thursday morning. The distant echoes of the firing didn't cause much concern—it was a familiar sound that often diminished after a few hours. If soldiers were late in receiving their pay, they would remind the government of their missed payday by firing a few rounds in the air. And it wasn't uncommon for students who were late receiving their monthly scholarship money to stage a riot, complete with gunfire.

Kevin had a meeting scheduled for that morning. Expecting that the city would soon return to normal, he decided not to change his plans. While he was gone Joyce received the call from the embassy.

A few minutes later, she received a second call.

"All Americans are advised to stay indoors," she was told.

Hearing the message on the embassy radio Kevin had with him, he decided to head for home.

What's going on here? he wondered, dodging potholes in the road. He could hear heavy firing coming from the main section of town. *This looks more serious than usual.*

*   *   *

At the International School in Brazzaville, teacher Carole Cook looked down at her watch, then out the window. She wanted to remain calm for the sake of the kindergarten and first- and second-grade children in her class, but was very aware of her rising pulse. Something was definitely wrong.

Parents began arriving at the school early to pick up their children. They reported hearing gunfire near their homes and seeing soldiers in the streets. And then Mr. Kim, the Korean man who ran the photo-developing lab, arrived.

"OK to take Youn Ki?" he asked, indicating that he wanted to take his son home.

"Yes, it's OK," Carole readily agreed.

Then in broken English Mr. Kim attempted to explain what was happening. He soon gave up his frustrating search for the right words.

"Phoom, phoom, phoom!" he cried, holding his hands as if he were firing a gun, his eyes rolling wildly.

What is going on out there? Carole wondered.

Not long after Mr. Kim left, Carole received a call from Mrs. Stubblefield at the U.S. Embassy, whose five-year-old twin daughters were in her class.

"I can't leave here," the frightened mother explained. "There's fighting going on directly in front of the embassy and I am not allowed to leave. I don't know how I'm going to get the girls. Can you stay there at the school with them?"

Carole agreed to watch the girls, but she didn't like the idea of staying alone with them at the school.

What is happening? Is Nelson OK? she wondered, her mind turning to her husband. She didn't know if he was near the fighting. She and Nelson had been in Brazzaville for nearly a year with the International Fellowship of Alliance Professionals. Nelson would accompany Carole to the school at 7:30 each morning and work with the kindergarten children for two hours. Then he would go on a "prayer walk" through the central part of the city before returning home two hours later. Since his retirement from the pastorate, he felt that his new calling was to a prayer ministry. When Carole was asked to go to Congo to teach, he accepted the challenge to make that country his prayer focus.

It was Nelson's favorite part of the day. In spite of the oppressive heat and humidity, he soaked up the sights, sounds and smells of Africa as he walked. He learned to avoid the cratered dirt roads, their perimeters heaped with garbage. With crows scattering, poverty-stricken people frequently sifted through the mounds, seemingly able to ignore the stench at least for the moment, looking for anything of value. Finally, when the trash heaps grew too large, they would be set on fire and burned down, and the dumping would start all over again.

Nelson loved to watch the Congolese as they went about their daily activities, observing their ways and practicing his limited French. He was amazed at the women and young children, their backs ramrod straight, balancing large bundles on their heads with apparent ease. He was also amused with the young children who were intrigued by the unusual sight of a white man with white hair and a white beard. Occasionally some child would venture to touch his pale skin and then scurry away nervously.

One morning Nelson watched a young man work his way up a thirty-five-foot palm with a strap circling his body and the trunk of the tree. After reaching his perch, with quick, sharp swings of his machete the teenager hacked off large bunches of palm nuts from which oil is extracted for cooking.

Continuing on, Nelson noticed a huge mango tree, most of its fruit having been picked before ripening. People often pick them while they are still green, he learned, in order to keep them from being stolen. Under the tree, a small commotion caught his attention. Two dark green lizards, each about a foot long, were fighting for their territory, their bright yellow heads glistening in the sun. Nelson appreciated what they did to control the bug population. *What would Congo be like without them?* Nelson wondered. *As it is, an African roach compares to its American cousin like a 747 to a helicopter!* he mused.

On occasion, Nelson's route took him to a spot from which he could watch the Congo train roar past, overflowing with people inside and out. Some stood on its roof—getting a free ride. Wanting to be able to move quickly, they chose not to sit, but balanced precariously in the wind. Even potshots from the police did not deter them from riding the rails without paying their fares.

I wonder where Nelson went today. I sure hope he got home all right, Carole thought as she made her way to the phone in the small office outside her classroom. BJ, her seven-year-old grandson, was close at her side. She called her daughter Bev, with whom they were living. Bev and Jay Bellamy were in their third year as missionaries with The Christian and Missionary Alliance. When the Cooks' apartment was needed for other missionaries two months earlier, they moved in with the Bellamys.

"Is your dad home?" Carole asked as soon as she heard Bev's voice on the other end of the line.

"Yes, he's fine. What's up with you?"

Carole explained the situation, telling Bev that Mrs. Stubblefield had asked her to stay with her daughters. "I don't know what to do," she added. "What's going on over there?"

"We have heard quite a bit of shooting," Bev told her mother. "But it's in the distance. Dad got home without incident. As a matter of fact, for no apparent reason he had made two diversions from his normal route and later discovered that there had been incidents involving groups of soldiers on the two corners that he bypassed.

"Something's going on, though," Bev continued. "Jay just got back from picking up Sean Hotalen. He's here to play with Danny for the afternoon. Anyway, Jay said the police are setting up roadblocks in the center of town. There was a lot of traffic and people were weaving in and out on side streets. But there doesn't seem to be a problem here—at least not yet. Why don't you check with Mrs. Stubblefield at the embassy and then bring the girls over?" Bev suggested. "I'll have Jay pick you up."

Carole readily agreed. She normally walked home from school with her grandson BJ chattering happily at her side. But on this day she certainly didn't want to be out on the street with three young children.

Carole quickly made the call to the embassy and spoke to Mrs. Stubblefield. Yes, it would be fine with her if Carole took the children home.

"What's happening, Grandma?" BJ asked, a wisp of worry crossing his face.

"I'm not exactly sure. But your dad is coming to pick us all up," she answered, gathering him and the twins around her to await her son-in-law's arrival.

*   *   *

Carol Erbst was exhausted that Thursday. There was still so much to do before leaving for the U.S. in two-and-a-half weeks—boxes to pack, cupboards to clean, papers to sort and many loose ends to tie up in her ministry. Her missionary colleagues had held a retirement party for her the previous Friday night and she was busy cleaning up her Brazzaville apartment just blocks from the Bellamys' house. She had spent thirty-eight years in Africa, the last four in Congo.

Carol was grateful for the helping hands of Anne Stephens. Anne's home was in Kinshasa, in the Democratic Republic of Congo (formerly Zaire), just south across the mighty Congo River from Brazzaville. Fighting in Kinshasa two months earlier had forced Anne and the rest of the Kinshasa missionary team to evacuate to Brazzaville. Since that time Anne had been living with Carol, assisting her in ministry wherever she could.

Carol was also glad for Zachary and Roger, two Congolese Bible school students who volunteered to help her with the sale of her household goods. People had milled around the house all day Wednesday and again Thursday morning, inspecting everything in sight. But this morning, as they rearranged dishes and lamps on the tables, they heard shots ring out in the distance.

"They're at it again," Roger quipped, taking a step back to admire his display. "I wonder what the fuss is about this time."

"I don't suppose it will last long, whatever it is," Zachary answered, straightening the shade on a lamp. "Things will quiet down soon."

Their conversation was interrupted by the telephone. It was a couple who had agreed to help at Carol's sale. Because of violence in their neighborhood, it was unsafe to leave their home.

"This might turn into something after all," Roger mused. Not wanting to think about it, he busied himself helping people who had come to make purchases.

As they were finishing up the sale, the call

came passing on the instruction from the embassy to stay indoors. Since Zachary and Roger were both from a neighborhood into which the violence was spreading, they decided to wait a while and try to go home later in the day.

*   *   *

Back at the Bellamys' home, BJ and Danny contentedly played with their guests Sean Hotalen and the Stubblefield twins. Running from room to room in their make-believe adventures, two-year-old Lauren trailed close at their heels. Mrs. Stubblefield called. She was anxious to pick up her daughters and get home, but she still didn't have the necessary permission to leave the embassy.

At sundown, the Bellamys were startled by the sound of soldiers banging on their gate. Bev and Jay caught each other's eye, unsure whether or not they should answer. They were greatly relieved to see their night guard, who had just arrived, go out and call to the soldiers.

"What do you want?" the guard asked.

"Turn off the lights," one of them barked, referring to the bright security lights that illuminated the wall surrounding the Bellamys' home. The lights were making it difficult for the soldiers to position themselves where they couldn't be seen.

Again, the phone rang. Mrs. Stubblefield had secured an armed escort to drive her to the

Bellamys' house and then home. She was on her way over. When she arrived a half hour later, she was very upset. In the less than three miles between the embassy and the Bellamys' house, she had gone through six roadblocks! At each one, soldiers had demanded to know why she was out, and at some of them had asked for money. She debated whether or not it was wise to travel with the twins, but she was anxious to get back to her house so decided to chance it.

Carole noticed she was wearing gold jewelry and suggested she put it out of sight. She agreed and shakily stuffed it into one of the twins' matching lunch pails.

"Please give us a call when you get home," Bev asked.

"Let's pray together before you leave," Jay volunteered.

The guard, noticeably uncomfortable with the responsibility of this frightened woman and her young daughters, seemed happier than anyone to have someone pray. Following the "amen" he quickly led Mrs. Stubblefield and her girls out into the rapidly falling darkness. He wanted to get them home as soon as possible.

The Bellamys were relieved to receive a phone call from Mrs. Stubblefield fifteen minutes later, reporting that she had made it back safely.

With two of their guests gone, Bev began to

make supper. Again, she was interrupted by
the telephone. It was Joyce McCabe. The embassy had called again: the advisory was now a
mandate. Because of increased fighting, all
Americans were directed to stay indoors.

Jay looked out the window. Another jeep full
of soldiers pulled up and the men dispersed
into the two-foot ditches bordering the road
and out of view into the darkness. They were
shortly followed by another jeepload. Jay
turned to look at his own three children and
their five-year-old friend Sean Hotalen, all of
them seemingly unaware of what was going on
outside. He whispered a prayer for their safety
and returned to the kitchen.

"It looks like Sean might be here for the
night," Jay commented to his wife.

"I think you're right," Bev replied. "I guess we
should call Stan and Connie and let them
know he's welcome to stay."

Stan and Connie Hotalen were part of the
Kinshasa missionary team who had been
evacuated to Brazzaville two months earlier.
Fighting across the river had calmed down
and some of the team had returned to their
homes and ministries in Kinshasa. But Stan
requested permission from the government in
Kinshasa to dock the boat he used for his
ministry and was told that the Democratic
Republic of Congo had not yet reopened its
borders for boats to return. So the Hotalens
had decided to stay in Brazzaville until they

were able to take the boat with them back across the river.

Again, Jay glanced at the children in their play. *Thank You, Lord, that they are oblivious to the trouble*, he prayed as Bev dialed Stan and Connie's number.

The Hotalens agreed that it was wise for their son to spend the night at the Bellamys' place. "You might have a little debate with him about that, though," Stan warned. "He's afraid to stay overnight at other peoples' houses. We'll be praying for him and you can have him call if he needs to."

"OK, we'll do the best we can and we'll be in touch," Bev said as she hung up the receiver.

Jay and Bev called a conference with the three boys. Their hearts went out to little Sean, who suffers with muscular dystrophy. They hoped he would understand.

"Guess what, Sean?" Bev said with all the excitement she could muster.

Sean looked at her expectantly.

"You get to stay here overnight. We'll make a pretend tent in the boys' bedroom and you can all go on a camping trip."

Sean's big blue eyes widened. "I don't do sleepovers," he said hesitantly.

"Well, we can't take you home right now, Sean," Jay explained. "There are soldiers in the streets and it probably wouldn't be safe for us to drive there. We talked to your mommy and daddy and they said it would be good for you to stay."

"That's right, Sean. They'd really like you to stay," Bev added.

"Yeah!" BJ whooped. "Hey, Danny! Sean's sleeping over!"

Sean wasn't convinced that he liked this idea.

"Supper's ready," Carole called from the kitchen.

"Come on, Grandma's got supper ready. Let's go eat and then after dinner, if you'd like, you can call your mommy and daddy and talk to them."

Throughout the meal Jay and Bev helped the boys make plans for their overnight "camping trip," emphasizing what great fun it would be. She could see Sean beginning to warm up to the idea.

"Do you know how to make hot chocolate?" he asked, his big eyes reflecting a hint of enthusiasm.

Bev smiled. "Yes, I do know how to do that."

"I'd really like some hot chocolate before we go camping."

"It's a deal!" Bev exclaimed, relieved that all was proceeding as planned. "Let's finish up with dinner. Then you can talk to your mommy and daddy, and then we'll make some hot chocolate."

A few hours, several cups of hot chocolate and a couple videos later, it was time for the boys to go camping. Two-year-old Lauren was already sound asleep in her room. But outside the barred and screened windows, gunfire was continuing to escalate both in frequency and intensity.

Bev and Jay herded the boys toward their room in the back of the house. Amidst flying T-shirts, shorts and assorted sandals, Bev and Jay changed the plan. The gunfire was very close. In fact, there was so much shooting behind the house that they didn't feel safe having the boys in that room—a stray bullet could too easily find one of them. Not wanting to alarm them, they decided not to tell the boys of the danger. Instead, they suggested having the camp out in the hallway. They didn't go on to explain that, in the event of a bullet hitting the house, it would have to go through two walls before it could harm anyone. And Jay would sleep with them. He began to move mattresses into the hall.

"I think I'll go home now," Sean declared.

Jay and Bev exchanged a questioning glance.

"We can't take you home, remember? Do you hear all the shooting outside?" Jay asked.

Sean nodded his blond head.

"That means it's not safe to go outside. And remember that your mommy and daddy said they wanted you to stay here?"

"Oh, yeah," Sean recalled.

"And Uncle Jay will sleep right here with you," Bev explained, trying to reassure their young guest. She, on the other hand, was looking forward to a comfortable night in their water bed.

Jay got the boys tucked in. It wasn't long before BJ and Danny were both sound asleep. Sean was another story. He was wide awake and ready to talk.

"How does this work?" he asked, looking at Jay's watch. Jay did his best to explain the mechanics of a watch on a five-year-old level. "Can I have something to drink?" "Why did you name your dog Larry?"

On and on he went, firing off questions, waiting for Uncle Jay's answers above the din of the machine-gunning outside. Three hours and dozens of questions later, Sean at last was overcome by sleep.

*   *   *

Sitting at his desk Thursday evening, Kevin McCabe made up his mind. As acting director of the International School of Brazzaville in addition to his responsibilities as Congo field director, he decided to cancel classes for Friday.

The shooting was not letting up as he had hoped. In fact, it was getting closer. Kevin still wasn't convinced it was anything more than a small uprising, but just to be on the safe side, he made the necessary calls to inform students of their unexpected day off.

Turning to his wife and daughters, eleven-year-old Shealyn and fourteen-year-old Shannon, he said, with a twinkle in his eye and more than a touch of sarcasm in his tone, "You know, the way this shooting is going, we just may have to be evacuated."

"Yeah, right, Dad!" they shot back.

"But just in case," Joyce said thoughtfully, "I think I'll put a few things in a suitcase." She took a large suitcase out of the cupboard and lined the bottom of it with their son Shawn's yearbooks from International Christian Academy in Côte d'Ivoire where he was finishing up his junior year. Large photo albums plus school pictures of their three kids followed. Joyce also carefully tucked her favorite African jewelry into a free corner—just in case!

*   *   *

Carol Erbst put away the last of Thursday's supper dishes. It was clear she and Anne were going to have overnight guests since there was no way for Zachary and Roger to get to their homes.

"Why don't we play a game?" Carol suggested, trying to offer something to take everyone's minds off the escalating uproar beyond the walls of the house.

Between telephone calls with updates from the embassy and from missionary colleagues, and times of prayer following each one, Anne and Carol taught their African friends some American games. It helped to pass the time and to calm nerves.

The evening wore on and it was time for bed. Completely worn out from two hectic days of selling and packing, Carol was asleep in no time. The others, however, stared wide-eyed into the blackness as the staccato of automatic machine guns echoed nearby.

Chapter 2

Wonderful Peace

Friday, June 6, 1997

L ess than an hour after Sean Hotalen fell asleep, the worst fighting of the night began. Around midnight, a bomb rattled the neighborhood, shaking the Bellamy house and everything in it. Jay shuddered and tried to get comfortable. It seemed every time he began to nod off he was once again jolted awake by the roar of automatic machine-gun fire. He arose early the next morning, his eyes still longing for a few hours of rest.

It wasn't long until the others in the household were up. "Did you sleep well?" Jay inquired of Bev.

"Yup. With all the soldiers running around out there, I figured between the national guard and the angelic guard we had nothing to worry about. Not to mention the comfortable water bed and how tired I was."

Gunfire broke the stillness of the morning, followed by a terrified scream. Jay looked out. Government troops were running down the street, yelling at the woman who apparently had been the source of the scream.

"What are you doing out here?" one of them demanded.

"You almost killed me," she shouted back, ignoring his question.

"You shouldn't be out," the soldier retorted, throwing the blame for the incident back on her shoulders. "Get back in your house and stay there."

The woman retreated into her home and Jay turned from the window. "Looks like we're inside for another day," he announced.

*   *   *

"How could you guys sleep?" thirteen-year-old Bethany Brown asked her family Friday morning. "Between the guns and the bombs, I was awake all night."

"I only heard one bomb," her sister Rebecca replied.

"I think we all heard that one," their father added.

Ron and Myra Brown and their daughters lived in the duplex next door to where Stan and Connie Hotalen were staying. It was right behind the post office near the center of Brazzaville. This was an area where, they would later find out, some of the worst fighting was taking place.

"I looked at the clock—it was right after midnight when that explosion boomed," Ron told his family. "It sounded like a canon!"

"I still can't believe that you went back to sleep," Bethany said, shaking her head. "I was awake all night counting bombs—twenty-four of them!"

*   *   *

Meanwhile at the McCabe residence, Joyce was in frequent telephone contact with the U.S. Embassy, trying to find out what all the commotion was about and how long it was expected to last.

Early the previous morning, Thursday, June 5, President Lissouba had sent his troops to surround the residence of his arch-rival, presidential candidate Denis Sassou Nguesso. Lissouba, Congo's first democratically elected president, had claimed the office in 1991 from Sassou who had governed for twelve years under the Marxist regime. With the national election coming up in seven weeks, Lissouba wanted to eliminate a potential source of trouble by disarming Sassou's private militia—the Cobras.

But Lissouba's plan backfired. Claiming he

had the right to defend himself, Sassou ordered his men not only to fight back but to go on the attack. The Cobras began targeting certain buildings, reducing them to rubble. Government forces fought back with abandon, trying to settle the score. Neither was willing to call a cease-fire.

By Thursday evening the international telephone lines out of Brazzaville had been cut, so news of the calamity was not reaching the outside world. Fearing that local lines could be cut at any time, the embassy began using its radio system on Friday instead of the telephone.

With the radio on, Kevin and Joyce McCabe could hear conversations between embassy personnel and monitor what was happening. The news grew more and more disturbing as the trouble spread. They heard that four French soldiers, believed to be spies, had been killed near the airport.

The official word to all Americans was that they were to stay indoors. The trouble had spread all over town. No one was to leave home.

Kevin's mind turned to the office, just three blocks away. If they did have to evacuate, there were things there he was going to need. He was no longer joking when he mentioned the possibility of evacuation to his family. "I think I'm going to try to walk up to the office and get the computer and a few other things," he said during a lull in the fighting. "Then if we do have to leave, things will be in some kind of order."

It was only three blocks, but it seemed like a mile. Kevin walked swiftly. The streets were empty. No horn-blowing taxis, no fume-belching transport vans that normally crowded the roadways. The few pedestrians he saw scurried along with their eyes fixed on their feet.

At the intersection two blocks from home Kevin came to a roadblock. Twelve government soldiers were there, stopping any vehicles that dared to be out, checking in the trunks and quizzing the drivers.

"What are you doing here?" a soldier barked at Kevin. "What nationality are you?"

"I'm a pastor," Kevin answered calmly. "And I'm an American."

"Lucky for you, you're American."

The soldiers waved Kevin by and he continued on his way mindful of the fate of the four French soldiers who had lost their lives earlier that day and grateful for his American citizenship.

Kevin wasted no time at the office. He swiftly tucked the laptop computer into its padded case and threw the strap over his shoulder. Reaching for the files he thought he might need, he whispered a quick prayer and headed out the door.

Shortly after Kevin was safely home a thunderous boom shook their house. Dishes rattled in the cupboard. Lights swung from the ceiling.

Kevin knew that sound. It was no longer just machine guns and other automatic or semi-automatic guns. The source of that boom was mortar fire from a small rocket launcher: the kind that could leave a very big hole in their house if it should find its way there; the kind that explodes on impact; the kind from which shrapnel flies with deadly vigor.

"Drop everything! We've got to go get Dr. Joe!" The voice of Ava Rodgers from the U.S. Embassy came over the radio, tearing Kevin's thoughts away from his weapons analysis. Joyce turned the volume knob in order not to miss any detail of the unfolding story.

Joe Harvey, a medical doctor with Global Outreach Mission, along with his wife Becky and their three small children, were in their first year in Brazzaville where they were study-ing French. It was the fulfillment of a lifelong dream for Joe, who had nurtured his desire to live in Congo since he was only six years old.

The Harveys were on Joyce's warden list. She had just talked to them on the telephone ear-lier that morning. They lived in a neighborhood with a high French population, which was not a safe place to be that day.

"They are taking everything that's not tied down around here," Joe had explained a few hours earlier. "I'm watching looters go by the house carrying refrigerators and everything else that's movable!"

Families were being turned out into the

streets. French mothers caught in this nightmare walked down the streets, grasping the
small hands of their terrified children while
crowds of people heckled and jeered. One fear-
ful step after another, they pushed their way
through the horror to the shelter of the French
Cultural Center two miles away. All the while
soldiers were firing wildly into the air, the bullets landing who knows where. It was a scene
of chaos and destruction.

When the soldiers had taken all they wanted
from each house, civilians picked up where
they left off. Homes were stripped right down
to doorknobs and plumbing fixtures. Empty,
bullet-riddled structures were all that remained.

As could be expected, it was only a matter of
time until Joe and Becky Harvey's home would
also be a target for soldiers and looters. Before
they had time to ponder that thought very
long, six soldiers came over the wall into their
courtyard.

"Give us money," they ordered. Joe fumbled
in his pockets while Becky and their frightened
children huddled in the hallway. Joe threw
some rumpled bills out the window.

"Now let's have the keys to the van," another
ordered, not satisfied with a little money when
a vehicle was sitting there.

As Joe stood wondering what his next move
should be, Becky heard their name coming
over the radio. It was the U.S. Embassy.

"What's happening out there?" Ava asked. "Are you safe?"

"There are soldiers here with guns," Becky explained, her voice trembling. "They came over our wall and they are wanting to come in and loot our house."

"We'll be right there—with the marines," Ava told her.

Becky shouted the message to Joe.

"The marines are coming to get us," he yelled out the window.

As soon as the soldiers heard that U.S. forces were involved, they ran. There were only five marines posted in Brazzaville at the time. They would have been no match for the government troops, but for some reason they fled. Perhaps they didn't know how few there would be; perhaps it just wasn't worth it to mess with the Americans.

Hearing what was happening, Joyce called the Hotalens and Browns on the Mission radio. The three families all held impromptu prayer meetings for Dr. Joe and his family.

Within minutes the bullet-proof embassy car packed with armed marines pulled up in front of the Harveys' home. Never did a sign of "home" look so good. Joe and Becky and their children rushed to the car. They were taken to the safe refuge of a Mission residence on the other side of the city. They knew their home was likely to be stripped bare in their absence, but that was unimportant to them at the moment. They praised the Lord for guarding their lives.

By that time the explosions and bursts of gunfire were getting louder at the McCabe house, though still somewhat distant. Joyce spent much of the day on the phone and radios, making frequent and repeated calls to colleagues and friends throughout the city.

One call was to a Dutch family living downtown where some of the fiercest fighting was taking place.

"Roland, if you need to get out, you're welcome to come to our house," she offered, feeling that in comparison to others, their home was still a relatively safe haven.

"Thanks Joyce, but there's no way we can get out." The tremble of terror was in his voice. "There are tanks parked on both sides of the house. We're trapped here. The Cobras have looted the brewery and are drunk. Some of them look to be only fourteen or fifteen years old and they're drunk as anything, carrying around these big automatic weapons. There's no way we can reason with them. There's nothing we can do."

Joyce had just hung up the phone when a terribly loud explosion echoed through the house. She picked up the phone once more and dialed the number of some close friends at the German Embassy, living only five blocks away.

After a few rings there was a strained, "Hello?"

"What's wrong, Torsten?" Joyce asked.

"We're lying on the floor. Didn't you hear that loud explosion?"

"Yes."

"It was a rocket. It blew up the house across from ours. Twenty feet closer and it would have been our place. We're on the floor."

"We'll be praying for you," Joyce offered.

"Yes, please do," Torsten answered. "There's nothing the German Embassy can do to get us out of here. They had a bullet-proof car but a group of drunk Cobras stole it and smashed it all up. There's no way we can get out."

*   *   *

As the hours passed at the Bellamy house, four young children played. The day was much more quiet than the night had been. Periodically, Jay and Bev looked out the window, but they seldom saw any soldiers. Then in the afternoon the racket started all over. But it was a different sound—the sound of heavy artillery. And it was close.

The volume increased. It soon became obvious that troops had installed a rocket launcher right behind their courtyard wall. Rockets were being fired over their house one after another, rattling the house and everything in it. It reminded Jay and Bev of the loudest fireworks they could imagine. Each blast was followed by yelling and small arms. But which troops were out there? The absence of government soldiers and these new and different sounds they were hearing made Jay wonder if their house was soon going to be surrounded by Cobras.

The children continued in their play. Every once in a while after an explosion they would stop and exclaim, "Wow, that was a big one!"

"These kids are in a state of divine oblivion," Jay commented to Bev, shaking his head. He was so grateful that God was protecting them from the fear and terror they could be experiencing. And there was no way that Sean was going home—another sleepover was inevitable.

"Sean, it looks like we're going to have another sleepover tonight," Jay stated.

"Well . . ." Sean said, carefully pondering the rest of his response, "I think I'd rather go home."

"We'll let you call your mom and dad again," Bev offered. "But you'll have to stay. It's not safe to go outside. And we'll make more hot chocolate before we go to bed."

"OK," he said cheerfully. It was settled—another sleepover it would be.

*   *   *

Carol Erbst put her guests to work all day Friday. She had a lot to do before leaving Congo and she had captive helpers. So she and Anne Stephens, along with Roger and Zachary, her yard-sale helpers who were still unable to return to their homes, spent the day cleaning and packing and doing other odd jobs.

The shooting came and went throughout the day. There would be a lull. *Maybe things are calming down.* And then it would start up again. *So much for that thought!*

"I wonder how bad this really is?" Carol commented as she wiped out an empty cupboard.

"Maybe we will actually be evacuated," Anne replied, mentally recalling her own rushed departure from Kinshasa only two months earlier. "I owe you some hospitality," she said with a smile. "You'd be welcome to stay at my house if we go!"

Night fell, and the cleaning crew went to bed. Carol was exhausted, but she couldn't sleep. Outside, the intensity of the gunfire punctuated with rocket explosions grew with each passing hour. Carol tossed and turned. *I can't sleep anyhow,* she thought as she sat up, *so I might as well get up and work.*

And work she did. She cleaned out her medicine cabinet. And then filled a box with her good clothes. Plowing through job after job until nearly 3 a.m., she finally fell into bed exhausted. And she slept.

*   *   *

There were no more jokes in the McCabe household about evacuation. The possibility now seemed more likely as each hour ticked by.

It was nearly time for bed.

"I'm sleeping in your room tonight," Shealyn told her parents. Never in her eleven years had she been so scared. She proceeded to drag her mattress into Kevin and Joyce's room. She then did the same with her sister's mattress.

"I'm not sleeping in here," Shannon protested.

"Yes, you are," Shealyn declared. "We're going to stick together in this."

Just before going to bed Joyce received another call from the embassy. "We'll call you every two hours with updates," they reported. Once again, Joyce called everyone on her warden list and told them she would not call throughout the night unless the situation changed.

Late that night, the McCabes crawled into bed. Joyce kept the radio where she could reach it on the stand on her side of the bed. Every two hours the embassy called. The message was the same: "Stay in your homes. Do not go out." And every two hours Joyce rolled over and acknowledged the message.

Between falling rockets and calls from the embassy, Joyce slept little that night. Awake once again in the wee hours of the morning, she got up for a few minutes. She walked to the living room and gazed out the window, her eyes following the path of red tracer bullets speeding through the night sky. She wondered what the future held, but there was no fear or panic—she knew the One who was in control.

Kevin too drifted in and out of sleep all night. Thoughts and questions raced around in his mind but he had a song in his heart. A deep peace flowed through him as God ministered to his heart with the words of the old hymn "Wonderful Peace":

> Far away in the depths of my spirit
>   tonight
> Rings a melody sweeter than psalm;
> And in heavenly strains it unceasingly
>   falls
>
> O'er my soul like an infinite calm.
> Peace, peace, wonderful peace,
> Coming down from the Father above,
> Sweep over my spirit forever, I pray,
> In fathomless billows of love![1]

Endnote

[1] W.D. Cornell, "Wonderful Peace," *Hymns of the Christian Life* (Camp Hill, PA: Christian Publications, 1978), #175.

Chapter 3

Plans to Leave

Saturday, June 7, 1997

B everly Bellamy hung up the phone.
"That was Joyce," she told her husband
and parents. "The embassy says we should stay
put, but let them know if we think we need to
be evacuated."

"Well, what are we waiting for?" Jay asked.

"I don't know," Bev responded uncertainly.
"How do we know what to look for? This is our
first term. I've never done an evacuation before!"

The night before, they had packed a suitcase,
but assumed someone else would be telling
them what to do and when to do it in case of
evacuation. A sudden burst of machine-gun
fire outside the gate put an end to the conversation. Bev rolled her eyes and smiled as she
handed Jay the receiver. "Why don't you call?"

Jay's voice was calm.

"Joyce, exactly what signs are we looking for that we should be evacuated?"

"What's going on over there, Jay?" Joyce asked, trying to read the inflections in his voice. It was 10 o'clock Saturday morning. Joyce had already received a recommendation from the embassy that morning that all Americans should leave the country. But how it was actually going to happen was still up in the air.

"There's shooting all around us," Jay explained above the din. "There's a rocket launcher in the school yard just behind our wall and last night they were firing rockets over our house. We think we are on the line between the Cobras and the government troops."

"I can't say for sure, but that sounds like it might be a real good time to call the embassy," Joyce advised.

Moments later Jay was on the phone with Ava Rodgers.

"Rockets were flying over our house every few minutes last night," he told her, wincing at another round of gunfire outside. "I think we're on the front line here—or very close to it. What should we do?"

"We need to evacuate you," Ava said, "and we're going to have to figure out how to do it. We haven't got anybody to send for you right now—and there are others who need to be rescued first."

Jay nodded his head, thoughtfully stroking his beard.

"Stay on the floor and sit tight," Ava continued. "We'll get to you as soon as we can. In the meantime we're working on a way to get you out of the country. There's an Air France flight leaving tonight for Paris. If I can get you on it, do you want seats?"

Paris? Jay thought. *That sounds awfully far away, awfully final.* "Yes, please, we'll take the seats," he said. If that was going to be the only option, he didn't want to miss it.

"There are eight of us here," he added doing a mental count of his family and in-laws, as well as Sean Hotalen, since he didn't know if they would be able to get Sean back to his parents before fleeing the country.

Jay's next call was to Stan and Connie Hotalen.

"We don't know what's going on here," he said. "It sounds like we might be going to France tonight. We'll have to take Sean with us to the airport—unless things change."

"We might be able to work something out with MAF," Stan explained. "I'm talking to Bill now on the radio—we'll keep you informed."

"OK."

"We might end up heading to the airport as well," Stan added. "But whatever happens, God be with you."

"Thanks, brother. And with you as well." Jay hung up the phone.

Bev looked at her parents.

"Happy anniversary, you two!" she said dryly. "What a way to celebrate forty-five years together—running for your lives!"

*   *   *

Stan's friend Bill Gillstrap a pilot with Missionary Aviation Fellowship (MAF), was across the river in Kinshasa. He had made a few flights between the two cities in the preceding days since things had calmed down in Kinshasa and missionaries were returning to their homes and ministries there. But his wife Tina and their two children were still in Brazzaville.

Stan called him and explained the situation.

"What are the chances of you and Ron bringing your planes over to get us out of here?" he asked, remembering that Ron Wismer, another MAF pilot, was also in Kinshasa.

"We'll do it," Bill readily agreed, recognizing the seriousness of the situation and fearing for his own family's safety. "You arrange to get all the missionaries and their families to the airport and we'll get them over the river. We've got a six-seater and a four-seater. We'll make as many trips as it takes."

"Thank you. We'll see what we can work out here," Stan explained, "and we'll get back to you with the plan."

Meanwhile at the McCabe residence, Joyce had overheard the radio conversation between

Stan and Bill. And at the same time she was on the phone with Ava Rodgers at the embassy.

"It looks like we're not going to need the seats on the Air France flight," she told Ava. "We've got a way over to Kinshasa. We'd rather go with that option."

"Ask the pilot if he's willing to take other Americans from the embassy. Or do they have to be missionaries?"

"Of course they don't have to be missionaries," was Bill's answer. "We'll take any Americans who want to be evacuated. They just have to get to the airport."

Ava agreed to the arrangement. The embassy would arrange a convoy to transport missionaries and other North Americans to the airport. Then the MAF planes would fly them to safety in Kinshasa.

"I'll get working on a convoy right away," Ava said. "Tell those pilots to come over and be waiting at the airport."

*　　*　　*

"What am I going to do if you leave me?" Michoue (MEE-shew) asked, unable to hold back her tears. "Am I supposed to stay here alone?"

Michoue was the Bellamys' house helper. She had come to work on Thursday morning, but shooting near her house had prevented her from returning home later that day. She be-

came another overnight guest with the Bellamys and Cooks, sleeping on a mattress on
the floor in Lauren's room.

Eighteen-year-old Michoue, recently married
and now pregnant, was very frightened. She
had tried to do some work Friday, but was too
afraid to concentrate. And she wouldn't eat.
She borrowed a French Bible from Bev and lay
on the mattress and read and read and read.
The mattress felt safe and the Scripture com-
forting.

Saturday morning when she found out the
Bellamys and Cooks would be leaving, she was
faced with a decision. Should she stay in their
house alone? Or should she take a chance and
try to get home, which would mean going
through the front lines of fighting and into Cobra territory?

Jay didn't know what to tell her. He doubted
she would be permitted to come with them on
the convoy. And he didn't like the other op-
tions.

"Let's pray," Jay offered.

Jay, Bev and Michoue bowed their heads.

"Dear Father," Jay prayed, "we ask You to
provide a way for our sister Michoue to be
safely stewarded out of this mess and to be reunited with her family. And Lord, please may
she be able to leave before we do so she is not
faced with this decision alone. Amen."

*   *   *

Meanwhile, Kevin McCabe spent most of the morning at the Mission office with Nicaise (Nee-KEZZ) the business agent. When it began to look like the missionary team was going to be evacuated, Kevin called on Nicaise to see if he could stay in their home and guard it, as well as look after Mission business.

When Nicaise agreed, Kevin took him to the office to explain various things and show him what needed to be cared for. He also gave him money to take care of expenses that could come up. The office was on the same property as the Center, so before going back to the McCabe's house the two men stopped to check on things there. The Brazzaville Center for Christian Studies represented the heart of Alliance mission work in Congo.

Alliance missionaries had entered Congo in 1992, just one year after its freedom from the empty philosophies of Marxist athiesm. The team had formulated a unique strategy. Nine experienced missionaries began the work with a nucleus of Christians, many of whom had come across the river because of uprisings and anarchy in what was then Zaire. They had established a small church in Brazzaville. The problem was they had no trained leadership. So the goal of the Mission was to establish a self-supporting Congolese church with trained leaders by the year 2007.

Learning from past failures and successes of The Christian and Missionary Alliance in Africa, the Congo team came up with a plan focusing on discipling believers and training leaders. Rather than building church buildings, they poured their energies into the Center—a place where their dreams could be turned into reality.

There's a saying in missionary circles that the Church in Africa is a mile wide and an inch deep. Too often it's true—the numbers are there, but a depth of spirituality is missing. The Congo team was determined to change that. They began a six-month discipleship course for every member of the church called "Master Life." It teaches believers to be accountable to small groups in Bible reading and memory work, prayer, sharing their faith, etc. Many of the fifty-six who graduated from the course the first time it was offered said, "I really didn't know what it was to be a disciple of Jesus Christ until I took this course."

In addition to the Master Life classes, the Center also became home to a library and a Bible school with both morning and evening programs. It was also used for Sunday school teacher training, Bible study groups, Sunday services and various other activities.

The 1996 General Council of The Christian and Missionary Alliance chose to direct its offering to the ministries in Congo, sending over $250,000 for the establishment of the Center. By May 30, 1997, the Lord had provided the amount needed for the final payment. The money was in hand, waiting for the previous owner of the building to pick it up. Now, with the sudden change of events, how would he get the money?

*   *   *

To their relief, Kevin and Nicaise found everything at the Center in good order. They also found Theodore, a young Bible school student who had been unable to get home so took refuge in the Center. Kevin invited him to come home with him and stay with Nicaise.

Their retreat through the deserted streets accomplished, the men sat down in the McCabes' living room to rest. Their conversation revolved around the fighting, each one voicing his speculations about where it could lead.

"Listen!" Nicaise exclaimed a short while later, motioning with his hand for them to keep quiet.

"To what?" Theodore asked, breaking the silence. "I don't hear anything."

"That's my point," Nicaise answered. "I don't hear anything either. They must be taking a break."

"You know, this might be a good time to get the Bellamys and Cooks out," Kevin mused. "Since the embassy can't get to them, we might as well try."

"Really? You're going to go out there again?"
Shealyn quizzed her father.

"I think we need to," he replied.

A brief discussion followed. "Let's go for it!"
Kevin finally decided.

They prayed together, and Kevin, Nicaise
and Theodore walked out into the unknown
once again.

Joyce quickly dialed the Bellamys' number.

"The guys are on their way up to get you,"
she told them. "They should be there in a few
minutes."

"Our bags are packed," Bev answered. "We're
as ready as we're going to get."

Bev called her family together and made sure
everybody had the one bag they were allowed
to take with them. She picked up Ruth Sterneman's laptop computer—that would be her allotted bag, while Jay carried the one with a
change of clothes for each of them and
Lauren's bag with the disks on which they had
backed up the Mission's records and other files
from their computer.

Ruth Sterneman, the newest member of the
Congo missionary team, had been evacuated
to South Africa with a severe case of malaria
only ten days earlier. For over a week Ruth had
suffered with a fever which climbed to 105 de-
grees. Too sick to be left alone, she had stayed
with Carol Erbst, along with Anne Stephens
and Marion Dicke.

While Ruth was in the makeshift hospital

room at Carol's house, Dr. Joe Harvey stopped in to see her frequently, administering medication and prayer. But her condition worsened. On Sunday, May 25, he left her bedside to interrupt the group of missionaries who had gathered for their weekly evening service. Walking briskly into the room, he stopped the music midstream to ask for special prayer on Ruth's behalf.

"If her kidneys don't start working in the next hour," he explained, "I'm going to have to call for a plane to evacuate her to South Africa."

While the group prayed, Dr. Joe went back to Carol's house to check on his patient. He joined in prayer with the friends who were constantly at her side. Within thirty minutes her temperature began to drop and her kidneys resumed functioning. But she was not out of the woods yet.

The next morning she was unable to keep her medication down, so Dr. Joe decided to administer it intravenously. In the meantime, the decision was made to order a medivac from South Africa. The plane, equipped as a hospital room, arrived complete with a doctor and a nurse.

Safely in Johannesburg, accompanied by Marion Dicke, Ruth spent the next four days in ICU. There were some scary moments, but slowly she began to regain her strength.

Since Ruth didn't need her computer for the time being, Bev had taken it home with her to install some programs and put other information on it. It was brand new. There was no way she was going to leave it behind when they left.

*   *   *

The Bellamys and Cooks were ready to go. When the doorbell rang, they wasted no time. Jay stopped to lock the door behind them and they were on their way.

When Jay realized that Nicaise and Theodore were planning to stay at the McCabes' home after the missionaries left, he recognized the answer to his prayer for Michoue's safety. She wouldn't need to stay alone. Nor would she need to cross into Cobra territory on her own. Nicaise explained that his uncle was a high-ranking government official and he would be able to arrange an escort for Michoue to get home.

The entourage arrived back at the McCabe home without incident, complete with Larry, the dog.

"When's the convoy coming?" Jay asked.

"It's supposed to be here around 12 or 12:30," Joyce said, glancing at her watch. "But I don't think it's going to make it, so we may as well have lunch. I've got spaghetti on."

"Enough for an army!" Kevin added.

Just then the bell rang at the gate.

"It's Pastor Aaron," Kevin said as he hurried to let him in. Pastor Aaron, the vice president of the Congolese Alliance Church, had come to see how things were going. There was heavy fighting near his home so he took his family to another neighborhood and then decided to check on the Center. Seeing all was well there, his next stop was Kevin and Joyce's house.

Kevin explained to him that the American embassy had recommended that all Americans leave and that they were waiting for a convoy to pick them up.

Pastor Aaron nodded his head as Kevin spoke, his deep brown eyes reflecting the urgency of the situation. "This is good," he affirmed. "You all need to get out of the country. It is not safe for you to stay."

Between serving and cleaning up after lunch and anwering calls on the telephone and radio, Joyce tried to pack her carry-on bag. There wasn't room for her to take the large suitcase she had already packed. It would have to stay behind.

The phone rang again. "Bad news," the embassy reported. "The Cobras have taken over the airport. We're not going to be able to evacuate."

*   *   *

Having received word Saturday morning to be ready to leave anytime, Carol Erbst and Anne Stephens had their bags packed and sitting beside the door. They slowly worked at a few projects, but couldn't get enthused about getting immersed in something they might have to drop at a moment's notice.

Carol arranged with Kevin McCabe that Roger and Zachary, the Bible school students who had spent the previous three days helping her prepare to return to the U.S., would be permitted to join the convoy until its next stop, enabling them to get closer to their homes.

Throughout the ebb and flow of the morning's gunfire they wondered if evacuation was really necessary.

"It's probably wise to go," Anne said, looking out the window.

"And we're likely to be gone only a week or so and then I can come back and get this place packed up and sorted out," Carol agreed, still thinking of the unfinished paperwork she was leaving behind. She looked at her watch. "Before we go anywhere we may as well have lunch while we wait."

They quickly fried some eggs, ate and cleaned up the dishes. And still they had heard nothing of the convoy being on its way. All that remained was to wait.

The phone rang again. It was Joyce.

"Sorry for all the delays. It looks like we'll finally be leaving here soon. We had heard that the airport was under Cobra control and we weren't going to be going anywhere. But that was a false alarm. They tell us that the convoy is on the way to our place. And you're the next stop. As soon as you hear the horn, come running—there's no time to waste."

The foursome decided to go outside and wait in the carport. Carol locked her apartment and followed the others to the heat under the carport's tin roof.

They hadn't been outside long when they realized the situation in the neighborhood was taking a turn for the worse. The sounds of battle were no longer muffled through walls. Gunfire roared from the neighbors' yard as a guard shot into the air. It was answered by more gunfire a few doors down. Both guns were then answered by the feverish barks of every dog on the street.

"I think they just want people to know they're there—and they're armed," Zachary observed.

A loud explosion cut off conversation.

Carol sat praying for her Congolese friends and neighbors. The volume in her carport was comparable to what most of them would be experiencing in their homes. She glanced at the tin roof over their heads, thinking about how easily it could be penetrated by a bullet. Faces of people with whom she worshiped and worked appeared on the screen of her mind's eye. Many lived in neighborhoods where the fighting was intense. How many had lost their homes or been wounded? How many had lost their lives?

She looked at Roger and read the worry on

his face. Were his wife and children in the middle of this? Were they still alive? Did he still have a home to go home to?

"Oh, Lord, please bring the convoy soon," she whispered.

Chapter 4

The Convoy

Saturday, June 7, 1997

A horn blew at 4 o'clock. After numerous unexplained delays, the convoy had finally arrived at the McCabe household. Quick farewells were exchanged between the missionaries and their African friends. Then the McCabes, Bellamys and Cooks scurried to the waiting vehicles.

Escorting the convoy was a military jeep with a mounted machine gun and six armed soldiers. White bullet-proof embassy cars were at the front and back of the convoy, their diplomatic flags flying. Between the cars were two twelve-passenger vans.

While his family and colleagues spread themselves among the vehicles, Kevin McCabe got into the lead car so he could direct the way to the other missionary residences.

Kevin was glad to see an army colonel in the vehicle. Even though he was not in uniform, his soldiers would recognize him and obey him, giving the convoy a degree of safety.

Already the vans were nearly three-quarters full with the families of embassy personnel. Nelson and Carole Cook squeezed into one of them with their five-year-old grandson, Danny, who sat contentedly on his grandmother's lap, looking out the open window.

Jay and Bev Bellamy got into the next van with BJ and Lauren and Sean Hotalen.

"I don't know if there's room back there for all of you," one woman cautioned, glancing to the rear seat of the van.

"There's room," Bev said. She immediately saw that some people had brought more than the allotted single carry-on each.

"We'll put the kids on the stuff and we'll fit everybody in." As she spoke she lifted one of the suitcases onto the seat and perched BJ on top of it. She sat beside it and Jay sat on the other side with Lauren and Sean.

A soldier came up and said something to BJ that he wasn't able to hear.

"What did he say?" BJ asked his mother.

"He said that if you hear gunfire or see people shooting you should duck."

"OK," BJ agreed with a nod.

* * *

The convoy moved rapidly through the almost deserted streets, stopping at two embassy homes before heading to the other missionary houses.

"We can't get any more in here," someone shouted at the driver. "We'd better go to the airport and the convoy can come back for the others."

"No, we are going to pick up all of our people," Kevin said firmly. "We are not leaving without them. We cannot!" There was no arguing.

The driver was clearly not pleased with having to continue. The fighting was more intense closer to the remaining missionary homes. Kevin reminded everyone that the embassy was responsible to get the missionaries to the airport since it was they who had arranged for flights across to Kinshasa. And so the convoy turned toward Carol Erbst's house.

They were stopped by government soldiers at several intersections along the way. The colonel simply got out of the car and said a few words to his men and the convoy was allowed through.

The driver of the lead car headed his vehicle down the road just a few blocks from Carol's house.

"Stop!" the colonel ordered. "Those aren't my soldiers," he said. A group of armed men were firing in the air at the end of the street.

"We're getting into dangerous territory here,"

he said, the tension of the moment creasing his forehead. "The opposition is really close. My soldiers may not obey me here."

"This is ridiculous!" the driver fumed.

"We have to keep going," Kevin stressed, his intonation stern and compelling. "We have to get these people. They've been waiting five or six hours for this convoy. And there are children there. We cannot leave them."

Amid firing and fear, the convoy detoured onto a nearby street and inched its way toward Carol Erbst's house. In the other vehicles people were getting increasingly upset. Those who did not have a relationship with Jesus Christ did not have the "peace of God, which transcends all understanding" (Philippians 4:7)— and it showed! One woman in the Bellamy van was frantic, yelling irrational instructions to the driver.

"Why is she so upset?" BJ asked, looking at his mother. "I guess this is a little scary, isn't it?"

Bev put her arm around her son.

"Well, BJ," she said, "we know that Jesus is in control and that He is with us, so we don't have to be afraid. But if we didn't know that, it would be pretty scary, wouldn't it?"

BJ nodded.

Finally, the convoy pulled up in front of Carol's place. Once again the sound of gunfire filled the air. The jeep that was at the head of the convoy whipped around to the back and the

soldiers jumped down into the ditches beside
the road. They shot into the air, warning the
nearby Cobra soldiers that they were armed.

"I guess this is what the soldier was talking
about," BJ mused. "Should I duck now?"

"It probably would be a good idea to put your
head down," Bev answered. But he was unable
to duck very low because of his position on the
suitcase by the window. He just put his chin in
his hands and looked around, more interested
than afraid.

Bev looked over at her two-year-old daughter
sitting on Jay's lap. She had no idea that anything was wrong as she chattered away, completely free of fear or panic.

As soon as they saw the convoy, Carol and
Anne dashed for the vehicles, followed by
Roger and Zachary who had arranged to ride
with the convoy as far as Browns' house.

"No! No! Not the Africans!" people yelled as
Roger and Zachary squeezed in. "This is only
for Americans!"

The reaction to her friends' presence told
Carol how serious the situation was. She could
feel the tension as she crowded into the same
van the Bellamys were in. Once people realized
that Roger and Zachary were planning to ride
with the convoy only to the next stop, they
calmed down and the convoy moved on toward
the Brown/Hotalen duplex.

"This is bad!" the colonel and the driver of
the lead car exclaimed repeatedly.

"One more block and we're there," Kevin said, trying to encourage them. "They're waiting for us and will come running out. Then we can get out of here."

A few minutes later the convoy stopped in front of the Browns' and Hotalens' places. The Hotalens with their children—eleven-year-old Jason, thirteen-year-old Christa and sixteen-year-old Jeana—crowded into the vehicles, as did Myra Brown and her daughters. Stan's and Connie's eyes lit up when they saw Sean safely in one of the vans, but there wasn't time for a reunion then—it would have to wait.

In the meantime Ron Brown quickly gave Zachary a tour of their house, showing him where he could find food. He introduced him to their German shepherd dog Coco, gave him the keys to the house and a radio with which they could keep in touch. Then Ron hurried to the waiting convoy.

All of the Alliance missionaries and their families were now on the convoy. Happy to be leaving that area of town, the drivers directed their overcrowded vehicles toward the airport. The remains of an exploded rocket lay on the side of the road looking like a twisted crescent roll can. The only people to be seen on the streets were soldiers.

There were several more stops at roadblocks, but each time the soldiers recognized their colonel in the lead car and let the vehicles pass without question.

The convoy was full. But pilot Bill Gillstrap's wife and children were yet to be picked up.

"We need to get them," Kevin said, feeling the responsibility for their safety. How could they leave Bill's family behind when he was the one who agreed to fly the rest of the Americans and Canadians to Kinshasa?

"They're just around the corner," he urged as they neared the airport.

"The convoy is already more full than it should be," Ava Rodgers explained. "And they're in such a dangerous area. We can't risk the lives of these forty-one people to get three more. So we need to keep going to the airport and someone can come back for them." Kevin reluctantly agreed, wondering how he was going to explain to Bill that his family had been left behind.

As the convoy approached the entrance to the airport they were stopped again by a barricade surrounded by a group of angry men. They appeared to belong to the Ninjas, a third militia supposedly not involved in this conflict. Some were in uniform, others in civilian clothes. All were armed. Four of them were wearing hats like those of French soldiers. The group's behavior appeared uncoordinated, illogical and irrational.

If these are the guys who killed the French soldiers, what are they going to do to us? Joyce McCabe wondered. *Is this where we're going to die?*

The colonel stepped out of the lead car and tried to reason with the young man who appeared to be their leader. He got nowhere.

Abandoning cultural expectations, the leader of the Ninjas showed blatant disrespect to the older colonel. While he yelled unintelligible threats, the rest of the group surrounded the vehicles. The van in the rear attracted the attention of three of the Ninjas—one carried a machine gun, another an antitank mortar and the third a crude hand grenade known as a Molotov cocktail.

More of the soldiers started to yell at the top of their lungs. They held their guns up to the windows, their red eyes casting menacing stares at the North Americans inside. It wasn't clear what they wanted. A flock of birds flew overhead, seemingly unbothered by the chaos and fear below.

Tension inside the vehicles rose. When one of the soldiers appeared to be messing with one of the tires of the van, an embassy woman began to panic. It was at this point when the difference between those who trusted in the Lord and those who did not was most marked.

Carol Erbst sat calmly taking in what was happening, trying to figure out what these drunk men wanted. Her mind turned back to a day three years earlier when she and a missionary colleague had been stopped by a similar group. That time their car was stolen. But in the middle of it all there was peace. Once again, as she watched these angry men surround the vehicle in which she sat, she had an inner peace that the Lord would see them through.

From where the Bellamys sat, they could see a flood of refugees carrying their possessions in huge bundles on their heads. Ironically, the road down which they were walking was called Peace Street.

"You know, BJ," Bev said, pointing out the refugees to her son, "those people are leaving their homes too and that's all they have left in this world. We need to pray for them."

"Wow!" was BJ's reply.

Jay's thoughts were racing. If there was one fear he had had about going to Africa as a missionary, it was what he would do if he were caught in a life-threatening situation. He had heard that the Lord gives peace in such circumstances, but now it was more than someone else's testimony—he was experiencing it for himself. There was none of the terror he thought he would have, though even at that point he expected they wouldn't make it. Watching the intoxicated men outside and thinking that he and his family and colleagues may all die within the next few minutes, he had a strong sense of the Lord's presence. Whatever happened would be OK.

Finally, without explanation, the barricade was removed and the convoy was waved through. No shots had been fired. The whole encounter probably lasted only five minutes, but it had seemed considerably longer!

Minutes later the convoy drove up the tree-lined boulevard, circled around the parking lot and stopped in front of the nearly deserted airport complex.

Bill Gillstrap was waiting to meet them. His eyes searched the four vehicles, looking for his wife and children.

They weren't there.

Chapter 5

Dodging Bullets

Saturday, June 7, 1997

A s soon as the convoy stopped and people began unloading, Kevin McCabe got out and went to where Bill Gillstrap was standing. He explained what had happened and promised to go back for his family right away. Bill nodded his understanding.

"OK, let's get the first load going here," Bill said, putting his own disappointment and concern aside and starting to organize the group for the flights.

As soon as he could, Kevin jumped back into the lead car with the colonel and Ava Rodgers.

"We're going back to get Bill's family," he said, giving them no option to suggest otherwise. "Let's go!"

A few minutes later they again faced the angry soldiers at the roadblock. Once again, they made no attempt to hide their rage.

"How many times are you going to go back and forth?" they demanded.

The colonel explained that they had one more family to pick up about a half mile up the road. Grudgingly the soldiers moved aside and let the car pass.

*   *   *

In front of the airport the North American refugees divided themselves into groups of three and five. It was going to take several flights to get everyone across to Kinshasa.

The Bellamys were in one of the early groups. They walked into the airport past a crowd of West Africans huddled in the wide entrance. These people had been led to believe that their government was sending a plane to pick them up. They had already been sitting there for two days.

Staffed only with soldiers, the airport lacked its usual bustle and excitement. Jay led his family through the international departures doorway into a bare room. They all filled out customs cards, then proceeded to the passport check. A soldier looked at their passports, then asked to see their proof-of-visa cards.

Jay looked through his wallet and handed the man a card.

"No, this isn't the one I want," he said, looking briefly at the card. "This doesn't do me any good—this is your resident card that belongs to the local police. You're at international customs."

Jay continued to search his wallet, beginning to get anxious that he couldn't find the right card.

"Is this what you're looking for?" Bev asked, producing her proof-of-visa card.

"Yes, this is the one. Do you have one like this?" he asked Jay, who continued to sort through cards and papers.

"This card is expired," the soldier said after looking at Bev's card more carefully.

"What?" Jay asked in surprise. "We have a three-year visa and we haven't been here that long."

"No," the man corrected. "You have a one-year visa and it expired over a year ago."

Jay's heart fell. *Surely we're not going to be stopped after getting this far!*

"Who are these children?" the soldier asked.

"These are our three children," Jay explained, "Lauren, Daniel and Benjamin."

"Benjamin?" he said, looking at BJ. "Did you know that my name is Benjamin?"

BJ knew enough French to understand the soldier's question.

"Really?" he replied.

"OK, I'll let you go and won't give you any trouble," the soldier said with a smile. "And when you come back, remember to ask for

Benjamin." Then, turning toward BJ, he added, "And you remember that your whole family got out because of you."

*   *   *

As the two MAF planes were loading their passengers, shots rang out nearby. No one knew who was doing the shooting or who they were shooting at, but it was unnerving. No time was wasted getting everyone seated with their seat belts fastened.

The planes took off within a few minutes of each other, while the rest of the group waited at the airport. From her vantage point high above the Congo River, Carol Erbst saw scores of dugout canoes filled with people fleeing from Brazzaville. Looking back at the far end of the city, she saw traffic moving and people walking down the streets as if nothing unusual were happening. *Maybe this is a localized thing after all,* she thought. *Perhaps it will blow over in a couple more days.*

On the ground Ava Rodgers, radio in hand, received another call. The Heineken beer company wanted to know if the U.S. Embassy could take a vehicle into the center of town to retrieve the six Dutch people employed at Heineken's Brazzaville brewery. In return they offered their ten-seater plane to take a group of people across the river for the embassy.

The embassy agreed.

*   *   *

Tina Gillstrap was scared. The rockets that were being fired from behind the Bellamy house were landing all around the house in which she was trapped with her two children. The night before, soldiers had come close to looting the house. They had even come over the fence, but then for some reason they changed their minds. Tina feared that it was only a matter of time until they would return.

She and the children huddled on the floor, wondering why it was taking so long for the convoy to come.

A rocket landed across the street with a thunderous crash. The house shook. "OK, kids," Tina said, mustering her last ounce of courage, "we're going to pray one more time." The three of them held hands and cried out, "Oh God, get us out of here!!"

A moment later they heard a horn blow outside. It was Kevin McCabe and the U.S. Embassy car. Their prayer was answered!

They ran out and piled into the car. Kevin quickly surveyed the area, amazed at the number of people on the street in spite of the firing. They reminded him of vultures just waiting for the Gillstraps to leave so they could hop the fence and loot the house.

A few moments later they arrived back at the airport, having once again passed by the drunken Ninja soldiers. Now all that stood be-

tween them and safety was a ten-minute flight
to Kinshasa.

The MAF planes returned and filled up for
another trip across the river. Then the Heineken plane returned for its employees who
were not yet at the airport. It was already
dark.

"Can someone get Ava on the radio?" the pilot asked after a few minutes had slowly ticked
by. "If she can confirm that she's got my people out, I'll make another run with you folks
and then come back one more time."

Joyce McCabe contacted Ava.

"They are all safely here at the embassy," Ava
reported. "I'm just waiting for a Congolese escort to take them to the airport."

When the pilot heard that, he looked at the
group of waiting missionaries—the Browns, the
Hotalens and the McCabes.

"OK, let's load up and take off," he said,
turning around and heading for his plane.
Thanks to his decision, the last of the Alliance
people would be on that flight.

"They were shooting at me when I was coming in to land," the pilot explained. "I could see
the red tracer bullets. But they're bad shots! I
think I'll take off without any lights on
though—just in case they improve their aim."

Moments later the dark plane taxied down
the runway and lifted off.

"They've adjusted their sights," the pilot observed. "They're shooting closer."

Looking out the windows the missionaries could see the bullets coming toward the plane.

"Hang on, everybody!" With that command, the pilot pulled the controls and the plane climbed steeply into the night sky, the tracer bullets falling well short of their target.

After dropping his cargo of missionaries in Kinshasa, the Heineken pilot returned to Brazzaville a final time for the six Dutch brewery employees who were waiting for him. Expecting that the soldiers would have readjusted their sights again, he stayed as low as possible when he took off. He judged right—this time the red trails of the tracer bullets sailed over the plane!

Between 4:30 and 7:30 p.m. the whole group from the embassy convoy had been ferried across to the VIP lounge at the Kinshasa airport. While they filled in forms so that everyone was accounted for, they were met by smiling faces from the U.S. Embassy in the Democratic Republic of Congo.

"Welcome to the relative safety of Kinshasa!" one said with a smile.

Chapter 6

Refugees without Number

June 8 - 15, 1997

Kevin McCabe woke early Sunday morning, June 15, to the sound of artillery across the river. The Brazzaville team had been in Kinshasa for a week and still the rockets flew and bombs fell. Even though the missionaries were twenty-five miles away from the river, in the staff housing of Evangelism Resources' School of Evangelism, the distance did not silence the chilling sounds of warfare. Kevin began to keep track. In less than three hours that morning he counted ninety bomb blasts.

"What is going to be left of the city?" he wondered out loud.

As it turned out, the Alliance team had been among the first expatriates to flee the battle-

worn city. With heavy hearts they prayed for
their colleagues in other Missions and their
Congolese brothers and sisters. Every rocket
explosion turned their hearts to their friends
and ministries across the river.

The day after their safe arrival in Kinshasa,
the missionaries listened intently to the radio.
The American Embassy convoy, attempting to
reach the Salvation Army compound had been
stopped by the Cobra militia. The tires on all
four vehicles were shot out and two hostages
were taken. They learned later in the day that
the hostages had been released.

Another Salvation Army missionary was
taken from her home with a gun to her head.
When her captor learned that she was an
American, she too was released.

The exiled Alliance missionaries met together
at least twice a day to talk about their experiences. Each had a unique story to tell. They
were also in daily radio contact with Nicaise
and Zachary, who were staying in the McCabe
and Brown homes.

"How are you doing, Nicaise?" Kevin asked
one morning, sensing a joy in his voice.

"Oh, pastor," he replied. "God has given such
peace. Theodore is here with me again after
being with his parents for the last few days. Today we were reading the Bible and praying together and God sent such a wave of peace into
me. It started in my head and went down
through me. Tears streamed down my face. I

have such joy—like I've never experienced before. Everything is falling apart around us. The noise is incredible—bombs are going off all the time—but I can really say that God is giving me peace."

Nicaise had been the first contact Kevin McCabe made when they moved into Brazzaville four years earlier. Kevin had gone for a short walk and stopped at a store. There he met Nicaise. Kevin introduced himself as the new pastor in town. Nicaise was quick to report that he was a Muslim.

"We'll be having a Bible study," Kevin explained, "and I'd like you to come."

"Oh, pastor," Nicaise protested, "I'd have to leave the cigarettes and the ladies before I could come to your Bible study."

"No, you come as you are to study God's Word."

And he came. Several weeks later, he showed up at the Bible study with a stream of questions. He'd seen the *Jesus* film and had been thinking things through. That night he received Jesus as the Lord of his life.

In the months that followed, Nicaise faithfully studied the Scriptures, absorbing all he could. After completing his master's degree in land-use planning, he was unable to find work. So Kevin invited him to be the business manager for the Mission. He'd proven himself trustworthy. So Kevin left him in charge when the missionaries pulled out.

"Pastor, this is turning into an ethnic war," Nicaise continued his explanation of events. "Theo and I should be enemies because we are from different tribes, but God has made us brothers."

Conversations with Nicaise in the days that followed brought more disturbing news. He was sitting alone one evening watching television when a bullet came through the roof and landed on the carpet in front of him right on the spot where Shealyn always stretched out to watch TV. Then a rocket landed on the house next door, leaving a gaping hole in the wall. And still he had peace.

Nicaise was one of six people who had remained in the neighborhood to watch over businesses and houses. He organized a coalition with the other five, and they frequently met together for encouragement.

"Nicaise, I never knew you were such a strong person," the doctor down the street observed.

"I'm not," Nicaise replied. "This is not me. If I were on my own I'd have been out of here a long time ago. It's Jesus working in me that enables me to have hope."

Kevin and Joyce were encouraged by Nicaise's testimony in the middle of the trauma.

"That is what the gospel does," Kevin said, turning off the radio.

*   *   *

African refugees escaping to Kinshasa found the exiled missionaries and came to talk and cry. They reported merciless artillery bombardment of heavily populated areas, house-to-house massacres of civilians from the "wrong" tribes, food shortages, rape of women, refugees trekking out of town by the thousands. Heaps of unburied bodies lined the streets, providing a feast for neighborhood dogs and rats. The stench was unbearable.

The stories came daily—tales of atrocities and suffering. Christians were not spared. They too joined the long lines of refugees fleeing the city on foot, taking only the few possessions they could carry. A deacon from one of the Brazzaville Alliance churches was stopped at a checkpoint and put in a line-up with four other men. The government soldiers accused them of helping the Cobras, then shot the first man in line. The deacon stood next to him, frozen with terror, waiting his turn to meet death.

Suddenly an army colonel appeared on the scene.

"He doesn't look like a bad guy," he said. "Let him go." He was freed, along with the others who waited in that "death row."

But some did not survive. A choir of thirteen women from another Alliance congregation in the city made it to the river's edge where they boarded a dugout canoe. Somewhere in the mile-wide expanse of swift currents between

Brazzaville and Kinshasa the canoe capsized. All thirteen drowned.

Would there be no end to the heartbreak? From the safety of their Kinshasa refuge, the Brazzaville missionary team listened to the continuing gunfire across the river. It was sickening—they knew those sounds meant that more people were losing their lives and more homes and businesses were being destroyed, crippling the city they loved. Their hearts went out to those for whom it was not an option to get on a plane and flee to safety.

*   *   *

"Hello, my friends!" The loud greeting came from Pastor Aaron, the vice president of the Congolese Alliance Church. Still in a state of shock, he came to tell the missionaries his story.

After saying good-bye to the missionaries and watching the convoy drive off that Saturday afternoon, he made his way back to his burned-brick house several blocks away. He was thankful that his wife was in Kinshasa and had been since before the fighting broke out. His two teenage sons were home—he hoped his two other children and granddaughter were safely with relatives.

For the next two days, Pastor Aaron and his sons sequestered themselves in the house. The shelling and rocket fire continued nearby. By Monday morning the noise was unbearable.

"Let's get out of here," Aaron said to his boys.

"Where will we go?" they asked.

"I don't know, but we need to try to get out of the city."

They walked out onto the street. Clouds of smoke rose from fiery buildings only blocks away. There was an eerie stillness, broken by frequent bursts of gunfire. They began to walk.

"What are you doing out here?" a soldier shouted, emerging from behind the ruins of a building. "Don't you know it's not safe?"

"We're trying to get to safety," Pastor Aaron replied. They were still only a block from their home, unsure of which direction to go.

"Get back inside," the soldier ordered. "Go back to your house and stay there!"

Obediently, Pastor Aaron and his sons retreated into their home. Nervous and dejected, they sat in their living room.

Suddenly there was an ear-splitting explosion. The house shook violently. Debris flew in their faces. A rocket had landed on their roof, blowing an enormous hole. Twisted tin and broken glass flew around the room. With hearts pounding, Aaron and his sons dropped to the floor, covering their heads with their arms.

As the dust settled they slowly rose to their knees. Their wide eyes surveyed what had been their living room. Deafened from the blast and too scared to speak, they stared in disbelief at the rubble around them. At last Pastor Aaron stood to his feet. Motioning for his sons to follow, he shuffled through dust and debris toward the bedroom. He directed the boys to crawl under the low bed, pulled other furniture around to act as a shield and then crawled under the bed after them. There they lay, unable to roll over, for the rest of the day and through the entire night while the shelling and bombing continued.

Rays of daylight finally filtered into the hideout, ending the longest, most uncomfortable night of their lives. Slowly they pulled themselves out from under the cover of the thin foam mattress and removed the barricade of furniture that surrounded them. They shook their heads, unable to comprehend the scene that met their eyes. The roof of the house was almost entirely gone. Only a few jagged points of broken glass hung in the window frames. Crumbled bricks were strewn haphazardly around as if pulled from their places by a hurricane.

"We must leave," Pastor Aaron told his sons. "There's no way we can stay here. There's nothing left!"

Kicking through the rubble on the floor, he sadly led the boys out of the house.

"Which way are we going to go?" one asked, looking up and down the street. One direction looked as ominous as the other. People were milling around in shock, not knowing where to turn. And rockets continued to fall.

"Let's head toward the road going north," Aaron decided. "It's the closest way out of the city."

They started to walk, picking up their pace as they went. Shooting continued all around them, but they forced themselves to carry on.

Still not far from home, they stopped briefly to talk to a group of young men. A few minutes later they bid them farewell and continued on their way. They were only a block away when a rocket landed. Looking back, Aaron and his boys saw the rocket explode right where they had been standing. All five young men were killed instantly.

Aaron encouraged the boys to face forward and keep walking. As they neared the city's edge, they joined up with other refugees—a staggering stream of people with only the clothes on their backs. There was a family ahead of them. Shots rang out. The mother screamed and fell in a pool of her own blood. She was dead. Her family had no choice but to leave her there beside the road and keep going.

Aaron and his boys trudged on. They were nearing the edge of the city. Surely they would make it. *This can't really be happening,* they thought. They were tired, hungry and in shock. But they wouldn't allow themselves to stop. They plodded alongside columns of others with bundles on their heads and the sick on their backs. They had to reach safety.

The cry of a newborn baby caught their attention. A woman had given birth on the side of the road. No one was there to help her. She lay exhausted, holding her newborn in her arms, sobbing quietly.

By nightfall Aaron and his sons were several miles out of the city. But they had no place to stay. So they slept beside the road. Cold and uncomfortable, they awoke early and continued on their way without breakfast.

As the sun rose in the morning sky, the three weary travelers were joined by several others. But no one had the energy to talk—they trudged along in near silence, mile after hot and dusty mile.

Finally, they rounded a bend in the road and spotted a village near the river. Its curious residents were anxious for news from the capital city. But there was no good news to bring— only tales of terror and destruction.

"How far is it from here to Brazzaville?" one of Aaron's sons inquired.

"Fifty kilometers," came the reply.

Fifty kilometers—nearly thirty-five miles! It didn't seem possible that they had walked that far in less than two days.

Pastor Aaron and his sons made their way down the rutted dirt road through the village, past mud houses and playing children. Women sat in open doorways, pounding roots in preparation for the evening meal. Chickens strutted to and fro, unaware of the strangers crossing their path. Pastor Aaron continued to the far end of the village where the waters of the mighty Congo River lapped against the shore. A group of men sat at the water's edge exchanging stories they had picked up from their fleeing countrymen.

The travel-worn pastor approached the group and asked if any would be willing to transport him and his sons, as well as some other refugees, to the other side of the river. One man was willing to make the trip—for a price.

Pastor Aaron gave the man the only money he had. They got into the dugout canoe and the boat owner guided his craft out into the swift current. With only paddles to propel them, the group worked hard and moved slowly. They were not far from shore when powerful waves began to rock the hollowed-out log in which they rode. Still they pressed on, their tired muscles straining on the paddles to keep the boat moving. Angry whitecaps beat relentlessly against them, threatening to sweep them helplessly downriver.

"Oh, God," Pastor Aaron cried, as another wave slammed against him, drenching him to the skin, "are we going to die here? You spared us and allowed us to get out of the city. Surely it wasn't so that we would drown in the river?"

For seven hours the refugees battled the waves and the current. Finally, as the sun slipped below the western horizon, they reached an island. They had no choice but to spend the night.

Pastor Aaron began to shiver. The temperature dipped into the 60s that night which, after the heat of the day, felt extremely cold. He and his sons wrapped their wet clothes tightly around themselves, but the dampness only seemed to draw the heat from their bodies. They huddled close together in a fruitless attempt to keep warm.

Aaron lay still, trying to get comfortable and not to worry about his other two children still in Brazzaville. He felt a sting on his hand, then his neck and face—mosquitoes! The dampness was attracting them by the hundreds. The small island was alive with hungry insects, buzzing around the heads of their helpless victims who felt as though they were being eaten alive.

At last the long night passed. Still exhausted, yet glad for the morning light, Aaron pulled himself to his feet. Turning toward the northwest, he gazed at the water over which they had traveled the previous day. As he watched the gray waves tumble and froth their way past the piece of land on which he stood, he recognized that it was a miracle they had made it as far as they did. He turned around, casting his glance at the water that was yet to be traversed. It didn't look much friendlier, though the distance was less.

"Dear God," he prayed quietly, "You have brought us this far. Don't leave us now. Get us safely to the other shore."

"Let's get going!" The canoe's owner was anxious to resume the trip. Pastor Aaron tried not to be afraid as he and his sons again stepped into the frail craft.

The last leg of their journey was relatively smooth—at least in comparison to the previous day's voyage. Finally the canoe owner delivered his weary passengers to dry ground in the Democratic Republic of Congo, a country that was opening its doors to refugees. It didn't take long for them to arrange with some soldiers for a ride into Kinshasa.

Pastor Aaron's eyes were wet with emotion as he poured out his story and his heart to the Brazzaville missionary team.

"I have never seen anything like this," he said shaking his head, "and it makes me so angry in my heart. These two leaders who are supposed to care for their country—how can they show no concern when their people are being trampled and killed?"

The missionaries had similar sentiments. But they had no answer. They could only share in his grief. Estimates were that over 6,000 people were dead. When would the murderous rampage stop?

Chapter 7

Black Thursday

June 16 - July 21, 1997

The exiled missionaries continued radio contact with Nicaise and Zachary several times a day. They were concerned about their homes, but even more concerned about the people whom they loved and with whom they had worked.

"Is Michoue OK?" the Bellamys wanted to know. "Did she get safely back to her husband?"

"Yes," came the reply. "She went to the village with her husband's family." That still didn't tell them where she was, since "the village" refers to anything outside of the city. But it didn't matter. She was safe.

Daily the team heard good news of acquaintances who had escaped the talons of death. And daily they had unanswered questions.

*   *   *

It was the afternoon of June 16. Ron Brown called Zachary on the radio for an update on what was happening in their part of town.

"Everything is still OK in your house," Zachary reported, "but yesterday afternoon I was scared that it wouldn't be for long."

He went on to explain that he had gone outside behind the Browns' house and found himself face-to-face with armed military men.

"Give me the keys to the truck!" one demanded, nodding in the direction of the Mission vehicle parked on the lot.

"I don't have them," Zachary explained, hoping he didn't look as frightened as he felt.

"Who lives in this house?" another asked.

"A pastor."

"White?"

"Yes. He's Canadian."

"What church does he work in?"

Zachary pointed to The Christian and Missionary Alliance logo on the side of the truck.

The conversation changed abruptly.

"Do you have any food in the house?"

"There's some rice. I'll give it to you if you want it," Zachary offered, his heart beating wildly.

"No," they replied, "we'll leave now."

Zachary stood there stunned.

"Thank You, Lord, for being with me," he whispered, as he retreated to the relative safety of the house. Coco met him at the door and licked his hand. He ruffled the fur between her ears, glad for her company.

*   *   *

Carol Erbst prayed often for Roger, who had helped with the sale of her household goods and the cleaning of her apartment. The last glimpse she caught of him was from one of the vans that made up the convoy—she had watched him disappear into a crowd of refugees. They were heading out of the city while he went the other way to look for his family.

The answer to Carol's prayers walked through the gate one afternoon at the Evangelism Resources complex where the missionaries were housed. There was Roger, standing in front of them alive and well.

When he got back to his house that Saturday afternoon he found it empty—his family had fled. He spent the night alone, amid falling rockets and heavy artillery fire. Sunday morning he woke early after a restless night. He wondered whether anyone would attend church that day, but decided he would go and see, just in case he might hear some news of his family.

As he approached the meeting place he heard the mournful wails of grieving people. Wondering what he might find, he opened the door and slipped into the room. What a surprise to learn he was interrupting his own family and friends who were mourning his death! Having heard nothing from him since early Thursday morning, they assumed he was one of the victims of this senseless rampage. Their mourning instantly turned to rejoicing!

A few days later Roger and some of the other Bible school students, along with their families, made it safely across the river in canoes.

Roger brought other stories from the disabled city across the river. The hospital across the street from the Brazzaville Center for Christian Studies had been bombed. While the Center remained undamaged, entire sections of the hospital were missing. Patients had been evacuated by any means possible, including wheelbarrows and piggyback rides. The staff failed to show up and there was very little care for any who remained. Government soldiers had put rocket launchers on the roof, which of course attracted return fire from the Cobras. Roger told the missionaries of a woman who had just given birth to twins and was hospitalized. "She too will die," he stated matter-of-factly.

"The city is destroyed," he continued, sadness filling his eyes. "Brazzaville is a village now."

The missionaries understood what he meant. Brazzaville no longer had the modern amenities one expects to find in a city, such as telephones, water, electricity and sanitation. The city was a wasteland. Yet, with seemingly nothing left to destroy, the relentless mortar fire continued.

*   *   *

The morning of June 26, three weeks into the war, Zachary radioed the Browns and told them that an armed soldier had come into the yard, threatened to kill him and demanded entry into their house. Zachary followed the thief from room to room and stood helplessly watching as he helped himself to their VCR, stereo and waffle iron. Only Zachary's pleading kept him from taking the computer as well.

"Pastor, I think maybe I should leave," he said, almost apologetically.

"Yes, you leave," Ron agreed. Ron had told him all along not to stay in the house if he felt that it was dangerous to do so. "Your life is much more important than our things." Ron also told Zachary where there was some money hidden in the house. Taking the money, their faithful friend buried the radio and the keys, put food out for Coco, gave her a final consoling pat and left, feeling it would be safer for the German shepherd to stay on her own than to wander the streets with him.

*   *   *

Nicaise remained as the only guard of Mission property. Although he was staying at the

McCabes' house, he was able to make brief excursions to the other missionary homes and the Center. He no longer slept in the house, but stayed outside all night with the other men who remained in the neighborhood to keep watch. With rockets still frequently falling all around, they decided they had a better chance of surviving if they were outside.

And so Nicaise spent his nights walking through the neighborhood encouraging others and praying for them. More than once he was asked to explain the peace that was so evident in him and he was able to share about the new life Jesus Christ had given him.

One afternoon Nicaise and another man decided to check on the Center and on the Bellamys' house. On their way they saw a rocket heading dangerously close to their path. Diving out of the way, they turned and watched it land on the school beside the Center. Machine-gun fire instantly answered the rocket's blast. Nicaise wisely decided to return to the McCabes' house and check on the Bellamys' place another time.

When Nicaise finally did get to their house two days later, he had only sad news to report. While he was there, armed looters came and took almost everything, including their vehicle.

"I did talk them out of a few things, though," he related halfheartedly. "I told them all your videos were American format and wouldn't work on their VCRs. They believed me and left them behind. And I also convinced them the computer wouldn't do them any good since it was full of Mission information. They took carloads of stuff and left. Later, they came back and took the furniture and appliances. There's not much left."

"That really stinks!" Jay said to Bev when the radio was turned off. "But I guess, in comparison to what so many of the Congolese have lost, our stuff is just a drop in the bucket."

Bev nodded her agreement. "But now I really wish we had given that typewriter away."

She was referring to a manual typewriter they had been advised to purchase before leaving the U.S. to use when the electricity was off. But the power failures in Brazzaville were short enough that they could wait them out rather than retype everything into their computer. And so the typewriter sat on a shelf unused. A month earlier they had talked about giving it to someone in their church but didn't know who to give it to so that others wouldn't be jealous or expect similar gifts.

While in Kinshasa, Bev and Jay had a visit from two students from their church in Congo who were studying at the Boma Bible Institute in ex-Zaire. (The Congolese referred to Congo-Kinshasa as ex-Zaire in order to distinguish it from Congo-Brazzaville. Neighboring countries both called Congo gets confusing for everyone!)

"We need to have a manual typewriter for next year," the students reported. "We have to type all our assignments and there's only one typewriter available for the whole school—so we can never get at it. And a new one costs $600!"

"If only we had known about this," Bev lamented. "I would have made that typewriter one of our family's carry-on bags." But it was too late.

"Do you suppose . . . ?" Jay wondered aloud, "Do you suppose that there's any chance that typewriter is still on the shelf where we left it?"

"It can't hurt to check, I guess," Bev said. "Let's ask Kevin to mention it the next time he talks to Nicaise."

The next day Kevin McCabe spoke again to Nicaise.

"The Bellamys have a question for you," he said. "Next time you get to their house, can you check and see if by any chance there is a typewriter on the shelf in their study?"

"No, it's not there," Nicaise immediately replied. "I've got it right here."

"Really?" Kevin was surprised. "How come?"

Nicaise proceeded to explain that he had stood in the Bellamys' living room watching the looters make a pile of their belongings on the floor. He saw them throw this black case, which he thought was an accordion, onto the pile. *These guys don't have any need for that,* he thought. When they turned their backs and went to help themselves to other things, Nicaise took the case from the pile and hid it.

When the looters were gone, Nicaise picked up the "accordion" and took it with him to the McCabes' house. He sunk into the couch with the case in front of him and decided to open it. And that's when he found out it wasn't an accordion after all, but a manual typewriter.

"God really is in charge," Bev declared when she heard the news. "Just think—when we were packing to leave the States four years ago, God already knew this was going to happen and He planned for us to bring that typewriter. And then He saved the thing from looters, for no apparent reason on Nicaise's part, so we can give it to someone who desperately needs it. Wow! There's no way that's just a coincidence."

*   *   *

Several days after Zachary left the Browns' house he showed up in Kinshasa, having made it safely across the river. He looked nearly starved and had many horrifying tales to tell. On his trip across the city after leaving their house he encountered fifty barricades. At each one soldiers demanded cash. He ended up using nearly all of the money Ron had directed him to take. With the rest he bought some bread.

He told of three traumatic weeks with only the dog and a radio for company. He was unable to eat—the constant mortars and shooting around the house kept his stomach in a knot.

The Hotalens had told him where to find a chicken in their freezer. He cooked it but couldn't eat it. The whole thing ended up as a banquet for Coco.

"When the shelling got the loudest," Zachary told the missionaries, "Coco came and laid under my feet."

Tears filled the eyes of Bethany and Rebecca Brown as they listened to Zachary talk about their pet.

"Sometimes I held her in my arms," he continued. "I buried my face in her fur—it comforted me until the gunfire let up. I was scared. But through all the noise and terror, I knew that God was there with me because not one shell fell on the property while I was there."

Zachary paused thoughtfully, regaining his composure before he went on with his story.

"I came to Kinshasa three days ago," he explained. "I went to my parents' house and talked to them most of the night. When they went to bed I couldn't sleep, so I just sat and stared into the darkness. The same thing happened the next night. Finally last night I got some sleep and was able to eat and get the strength to come and find you."

*   *   *

Thursday, July 3, 1997, will probably always be remembered by Ron and Myra Brown and their daughters as "Black Thursday." That is when they received word from Nicaise that, for the second time in six years, they lost all their household goods. Back to zero again.

The duplex they had called home was in deplorable condition. The gates were swinging in the wind, the doors were shot open, broken glass was littered inside and out, a handful of books and papers were strewn on the office floor. Only a few items of heavy furniture remained, the rest was gone.

And Nicaise had more upsetting news. He had found Coco curled up in a cardboard box in a back bedroom, traumatized. He gave her food, but wasn't sure she would eat it.

The Browns had hoped and prayed that the news would be otherwise. Many of the stolen things were replaceable, but some were not. At least their Toyota four-wheel-drive wasn't in their yard or it would be gone too. Two months earlier they had had a fender bender and had taken their vehicle to the body shop for repairs. Two days before the evacuation Ron had stopped by to check the progress on it. The car was dismantled—the bumper had been removed, and the repaired fender sat on a table where it was being painted.

"I wonder if we dare hope the Toyota is still at the shop?" Ron thought out loud.

*   *   *

News continued to trickle across the river from Brazzaville to Kinshasa where the exiled missionaries waited and wondered what their next step would be. They mourned the loss of their ministries and life as they knew it. A month had passed since the war had broken out and still the ammunition flew. Four cease-fires had been called, but all were broken nearly as soon as they were announced. Did anyone in Brazzaville understand the meaning of the term?

Ruth Sterneman and Marion Dicke arrived safely in Kinshasa from South Africa. Though still lacking some strength, Ruth had recovered from her bout with malaria. Had she not been ill, she would have moved into an area of Brazzaville that turned out to be a hot spot in the war. Once again, God reminded Ruth and her colleagues that He was watching out for them even before they knew there was a problem.

Nicaise continued to call on the radio with updates. He paid a visit to the garage where the Browns had left their vehicle for repairs. The garage had been looted and stood empty.

Large sections of the city, including the McCabes' neighborhood, were without water and electricity.

"You had better eat up the food in the freezer," Kevin instructed Nicaise. "Cook up whatever you can find and have a block party!" There were only five people left on the block, so they would have to do a lot of eating. Kevin remembered the twelve-pound turkey in the freezer for which he had paid $52! *Oh well, that's the way it goes!* he thought.

The U.S. Embassy had pulled out of Brazzaville. Some days the fighting was so intense that explosions rattled windows in Kinshasa, two miles away across the broad Congo River. Other days were relatively quiet. But just when the missionaries began to think things were calming down, the shooting started all over again. It was looking less and less likely that the Mission would be able to resume its ministries in Brazzaville in the near future.

"Don't even try to come back now," Nicaise warned. "There are no white people around at all—to have a white face is to be a target." The missionaries began checking into returning to their homes in the U.S. and Canada.

News from other sources told of the Red Cross trying to pick up the dead and distribute medicines. There were reports of widespread dysentery and other illnesses, and with no water and electricity in much of the city, the Red Cross was afraid of a health crisis. They managed to collect hundreds of bodies from the streets before their efforts were suspended in the face of increased fighting.

People continued to flee from the city. Food became more and more scarce—and more and more expensive. Gas stations were destroyed and it was reported that soldiers were using buckets to dip fuel from open reserves in the ground.

President Lissouba and Denis Sassou Nguesso were in Libreville, the capital city of neighboring Gabon, where negotiations for peace were supposedly taking place. But little or no progress was being made.

There were occasional bits of encouraging news that reached the missionaries' ears. On July 17 Nicaise called with such a report.

"There was a big party yesterday," he told them. "In three different places in the city, Cobras and government soldiers said to each other, 'This is ridiculous! Our leaders are not going to stop this until all of our families are dead. Let's stop fighting.' And so they put down their guns and had an all-day party.

"Then today there was a huge convoy," Nicaise continued. "Soldiers from both sides, riding in about fifty vehicles, drove through the city telling the people to stop fighting. 'Our leaders sent all their children to safety in Europe,' they said. 'It's *our* children who are dying. Let's stop fighting for them.' "

Such reports were encouraging, bringing glimmers of hope that the war might soon be over. But the encouragement was short-lived. Within a few hours of sharing in Nicaise's excitement, the Brazzaville missionary team again heard blasts coming from across the river.

After more than a month of waiting and with no end to the war in sight, the missionaries, in conjunction with Mission leadership in the U.S. and Canada, made the decision to return to their homes in North America. By July 21, 1997, the entire Brazzaville team was back on North American soil, with the exception of Ruth Sterneman, who stayed in Kinshasa to continue her study of the Lingala language.

Chapter 8

God Is Good—
All the Time

August 1997 - February 1998

K evin McCabe sat on the porch of his Western Pennsylvania home sipping a tall glass of iced tea and enjoying the stillness of the small-town evening. Fireflies danced through the flower beds and across the neatly manicured yard. Cricket songs filled the air. Neighborhood children ran past, their laughter bringing a smile to his face.

Kevin let out a heavy sigh as he raked his fingers through his graying hair. The McCabes had been home less than a month, and even though the war in Brazzaville raged on, they were already contemplating returning to Africa. Earlier that day, he had been in contact with missionary colleague Jim Sawatsky in Kinshasa. Jim had informed him of ministry possibilities there in which he and Joyce could use their teaching gifts. Should they accept his invitation?

Kevin was already planning to return to Africa at the end of August to enroll seventeen-year-old Shawn and fourteen-year-old Shannon for the fall trimester at the International Christian Academy in Côte d'Ivoire. And then he hoped to visit Kinshasa and maybe even make a trip to Brazzaville. But should Joyce and eleven-year-old Shealyn go with him?

Being in Kinshasa would enable them to keep tabs on the situation across the river in Brazzaville and they'd be ready to move back in as soon as it was feasible to do so. On the other hand, it would be comfortable to stay in Pennsylvania for a while. They had enjoyed spending time with both sets of parents, as well as brothers and sisters, nieces and nephews.

Joyce pulled up a chair and joined Kevin on the porch.

"It's more than just a job we're talking about here," he said as Joyce sat down. "This is a calling from God."

Joyce nodded her agreement. She felt the same way. They had already talked to their children about it and all three were in favor of moving back across the Atlantic Ocean once again.

"I don't believe our work there is finished," Joyce said softly.

"Neither do I," Kevin whispered. He thought for a moment before adding, "It's just the beginning of another chapter. I wonder what this chapter will hold."

It was settled. Kevin returned to Africa on August 25, dropping Shawn and Shannon off in Côte d'Ivoire and carrying on to Kinshasa. Joyce and Shealyn joined him there three weeks later.

*   *   *

Back in Kinshasa, the capital city of ex-Zaire, the McCabes could once again hear the gunfire and rocket blasts across the river, pounding at the heart of Brazzaville. The news coming out of Brazzaville was no better than it had been when they left for the U.S. nearly two months earlier. Radio contact with Nicaise, who was still staying in their house, filled them in on the latest events of the battle. With government troops dropping rockets from helicopters, more of the city center was being blown away each day. Food was scarce and the little that was available was expensive. Aid workers estimated that only five to ten percent of the city's 800,000 residents remained. Young Cobra soldiers patrolled the empty streets, armed with weapons they didn't know how to use.

Kevin asked Nicaise about the Mission properties.

"The Bellamy house took a hit from a large

mortar," he explained. "The fire burned for quite a while afterward. The house is in bad shape."

"What about the Center?" Kevin inquired.

"It still stands unharmed!" Nicaise excitedly told him. "Some military guys went upstairs there one day. I assumed they were looking for what they could steal. All they saw were books so they left."

"Praise the Lord!" Kevin exclaimed.

"Yes, pastor, it is like Shawn said: 'God is good—all the time!' "

Kevin smiled at the memory. In the first e-mail message he and Joyce received from their son Shawn after they had been evacuated from Brazzaville, they read, "Remember, God is good—all the time!" Kevin was glad that Nicaise was able to see God's goodness in the middle of the terrible circumstances all around him.

A few days later Nicaise reported that the McCabes' dog had been hit by a stray bullet and had died. "Mighty Larry," the Bellamys' white poodle, was now his only remaining canine companion.

The next morning Nicaise radioed with the news that the McCabes' house had been hit by a rocket bomb.

"Praise the Lord for His timing," he said. "I went down the street at 10 o'clock to order food from the truck driver who goes by every morning. When I got back here, I saw that the house had been hit." Nicaise went on to explain that the bomb came through the roof into the dining room and exploded. The casing flew through a wall, ending up in the front yard.

"If I had been here when the bomb hit," Nicaise said thoughtfully, "I probably would have been killed. But God protected me."

*   *   *

It didn't take long for Kevin and Joyce to dig into ministry, each of them teaching a course at Evangelism Resources' School of Evangelism. They were also involved with relief efforts on behalf of Congolese refugees. The Alliance people in Kinshasa began the job on their knees, inviting Christians to gather for prayer for Brazzaville and the people who had fled its devastation. Pastors Aaron and Omer from the Brazzaville Alliance Church, as well as the director of World Vision for the region, took part in the service.

It concluded with an offering which had been announced in advance, so people came prepared to give, even though they themselves were living in poverty. Piles of clothes, soap, medicine and money accumulated at the front of the auditorium. A group of Christian doctors had agreed to take the gifts into Brazzaville the next day.

A handicapped man crawling up the aisle caught Kevin's attention. Inching his way forward, dragging a sack of his belongings, the man kept his eyes fixed at the front. Beads of sweat formed on his forehead as the crowd watched him add his sacrificial gift to the pile. The congregation, many with tears falling unashamedly down their faces, burst into spontaneous applause. God was definitely working among them.

Kevin and Joyce made frequent visits to Kinkole refugee camp with Pastor Aaron and others. Kinkole, the largest camp in the area, was established in the sandy hills twenty miles southeast of Kinshasa. In the month of September its population grew from 6,000 to over 38,000.

As Kevin toured the camp, visiting in the scant shade of the plastic huts sheltering people from the blazing sun, he was keenly aware of their suffering. Through a thin veneer of optimism, he could see in their eyes the fear and sadness that engulfed their hearts.

"I have been separated from my five children for nearly three months," one woman told him, her dark eyes clouded with grief. "I don't even know if they are alive. . . ." She paused to regain her composure. "And I have no way to find them."

Teachers and businessmen, nurses and janitors lived side by side, sharing their meager possessions. No longer separated by social status, they stood together on the level ground of homelessness.

Five organizations were working in the camp, among them the World Health Organization and Doctors Without Borders. Things were well organized for temporary housing and the distribution of food and water. Vaccinations were being given to control the outbreak of cholera and measles in the camp. But Kevin could find no evidence of any spiritual help being offered.

A group of evangelical pastors in Kinshasa began to organize Sunday services. They erected a makeshift chapel by stretching several sheets of plastic between poles. The simple facilities and lack of seating didn't deter people from attending. Large crowds gathered to sing and hear teaching from God's Word.

The Christians sought permission from the camp administration to show the *Jesus* film. It was granted.

The film was shown on two separate occasions on a huge screen visible to hundreds of people. Hungry, grieving, unemployed and homeless, they came to hear about the man named Jesus. They saw His compassion for hurting people. They saw how He was unfairly crucified, then raised back to life. They were told that His death was to pay for their sins and that He came to bring forgiveness and peace. Congolese Christians were living examples of the peace in turmoil that only Jesus can offer. Wanting that peace for themselves, over 200 people committed their lives to Christ in one meeting.

*   *   *

Several rounds of peace talks between Congo's opposing leaders failed to bring any lasting changes. Machine-gun fire still rattled through the streets, each side vying for the leading edge in the four-month power struggle.

Finally, on October 15, 1997, with President Lissouba's whereabouts unknown, his arch-rival's Cobra militia marched into the capital and claimed control of the Republic of Congo. Heavily armed, many of them guzzling beer, they made their way to the presidential palace and began emptying it of its contents. As they piled goods into waiting trucks, they accused Lissouba of being responsible for the whole civil war. He deserved to have his residence plundered, they argued.

Cobra troops, with the help of the Angolan military, also took control of Point Noire, Congo's second largest city. According to Red Cross reports, only twenty lives were lost in that encounter.

Cobra leader Denis Sassou Nguesso, raising a glass of champagne to his lips, declared victory over Lissouba. He was later greeted with a hero's welcome in his hometown.

Occasional shots still echoed through the once impressive center of Brazzaville. But the war was over, leaving bodies strewn along the tree-lined streets. An accurate count of the dead was impossible since many of the victims

had been hastily buried, burned or thrown into the Congo River. Others had been devoured by wild dogs. The city was virtually destroyed. Buildings which only four months earlier had housed successful businesses now stood as empty skeletons, silent witnesses to weeks of fierce fighting.

*   *   *

Over a month had gone by since Kevin and Joyce McCabe had heard from Nicaise. After the bomb fell on their house, they had encouraged him to leave and find safety elsewhere. The last they heard from him was that he was going to seek advice from his uncle and would call the McCabes back later that day with his decision. He never called back.

After weeks of silence and wondering what was happening across the river, Kevin planned a weekend excursion into the city that he and his family had called home for three years.

Early Friday morning, November 14, Kevin took a taxi down to the beach and boarded a ferry. As the boat hummed and rocked its way over the waves, Kevin stared ahead, trying to prepare himself for what he might see. He could already recognize the Elf Oil Tower and the Sofitel Hotel, both structures blackened from their encounters with bombs and fires.

Cobra militiamen met Kevin at the Brazzaville beach. They looked at his passport and directed him to an office where he was required to sign in on different lists and pay various fees.

"Why all this money?" Kevin asked, handing over $8.

"We haven't been paid," a young soldier answered. "This is for our salaries."

Finally through the beach gates, Kevin headed toward the center of town. Everywhere he looked, he saw the evidence of war—even at his feet where it seemed the pebbles had been replaced by empty shells. Thousands of them littered the streets.

Rounding the corner by the Russian Embassy, he stopped and tried to take in the sights and smells of the destroyed city. On his left stood the skeleton of the Elf Oil Tower, once a symbol of progress and national pride. Gaping holes replaced the copper-tinted windows which now lay in thousands of pieces around the great building's feet.

On his right were the charred remains of the Gurhnam store. Happy memories flooded Kevin's mind. He thought of the people who had worked there, remembering shared jokes and casual conversations over grocery carts.

Brazzaville will never be the same, he thought sadly as he walked on.

An eerie feeling came over him as he continued down the street. A group of people were rooting through the presidential headquarters for the election that was to have been held in

Kevin and Joyce McCabe. As Congo field director, Kevin felt responsible to get his colleagues to safety. Joyce served as a warden to relay messages from the U.S. Embassy to American citizens.

CONGO

At the time of the evacuation, Carole and Nelson Cook had been in Congo for nearly a year with the International Fellowship of Alliance Professionals.

Ron and Myra Brown lost all of their belongings for the second time in six years.

Jay and Beverly Bellamy, with BJ, Danny and Lauren. Though rockets were being fired over their house, the Bellamy children contentedly played, seemingly oblivious to the commotion.

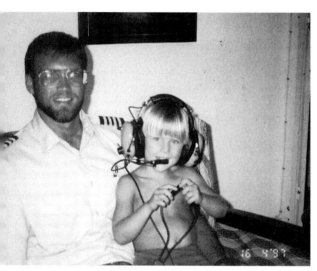

MAF pilot Bill Gillstrap with five-year-old Sean Hotalen. Bill was one of three pilots who flew the missionary team across the Congo River to safety in Kinshasa.

Carol Erbst and Ruth Sterneman. Carol was evacuated from Congo just two weeks before she was to leave for retirement. Ten days earlier Ruth had been evacuated to South Africa with a serious case of malaria.

Stan Hotalen used this boat for evangelism in Teke villages along the wide Congo River.

Brazzaville, on the shores of the Congo River, once boasted an impressive city center with tree-lined streets and modern buildings.

The Ron Brown family in a dug-out canoe. Refugees fled war-torn Brazzaville in canoes like this one. Many reached safety on the other side—others did not.

Bible school students in a chapel service at the Brazzaville Center for Christian Studies. These students were scattered by the war.

One of the hardest losses for Rebecca Brown and her sister Bethany was not knowing what happened to Coco, their German shepherd.

Hundreds of refugees came to Christ through worship services and evangelism at Kinkole refugee camp on the outskirts of Kinshasa.

Mission Aviation Fellowship volunteered the services of their two planes in Kinshasa to evacuate missionaries and other North Americans from Brazzaville.

This duplex was home to the Brown and Hotalen families
at the time of the evacuation.

Looters left nothing but trash strewn throughout the Brown family's house.

Back in Brazzaville in January 1998 to survey the damage, Joyce McCabe stepped carefully through the rubble in Lauren Bellamy's burned-out bedroom where a rocket had landed and blown away the roof.

Nicaise, business manager for the Mission, experienced God's peace and joy while bombs were falling around him. His powerful witness demonstrated to others in the neighborhood what God can do in a life yielded to Him.

Bob Fetherlin, Alliance Regional Director for Africa, joins Kevin and Joyce McCabe looking for anything salvageable in a bedroom of David and Tammy Noels' house (occupied at the time by the Hotalen family).

The Brazzaville Center for Christian Studies stood unharmed through four months of civil war. The buildings on all four sides of it suffered heavy damage.

The picture says it all!

Don and Esther Weidemann, Cambodia field director. Though they could hear the fighting, Don and Esther's home was a "safe" distance from the front line.

Fire in a nearby neighborhood gave Marie Ens opportunity for ministry by meeting the needs of homeless families.

A rocket exploded in David and Doris Strong's front yard.

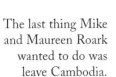

The last thing Mike and Maureen Roark wanted to do was leave Cambodia.

Left: Steve and Mary Westergren with Eric, Kirsten, Brent and Kreg spent five terrifying hours on the floor in Steve's office.

Right: David and Chris Manfred with Joshua, Joel and Janelle were "evaporated" safely across the Thai border.

From their kitchen window, Mike and Maureen Roark watched smoke rise from the remains of three homes destroyed by a rocket.

Bill and Ilana Lobbezoo were thankful that two-year-old Holly slept soundly through the worst of the fighting near their home.

Bounoeuy and Chanthan Kes with Diana and Sammy. Bounoeuy fled Cambodia as a teenager in 1979 and returned as a missionary eleven years later.

Mike Roark tries to cross one of Phnom Penh's crowded down-town streets.

The Killing Fields Memorial building (insert) is stacked full of skulls from people cruelly executed during the Pol Pot regime.

Over 100 small thatch, wood and cardboard houses were completely wiped out by falling rockets and fire. The Roarks and Marie Ens had friends whose homes in the area remained intact despite the surrounding devastation.

Mike and Maureen Roark live in the upstairs apartment of this home belonging to a cabinet minister in the Cambodian government.
The Roarks watched as defecting soldiers sat and smoked cigarettes on the steps leading to their apartment. The soldiers then changed into civilian clothes, hid their weapons and casually walked out of the yard and onto the street.

An armored personnel carrier (center of picture)
sat on Dike Road, which became the front line
of the battle, not far from missionary residences.

With only one carry-on bag allowed per person, the missionaries
gather to check in at Pochentong International Airport.

Because the airport terminal was heavily damaged, evacuees waited with hundreds of others under this shelter to receive their boarding passes, pay an airport tax and have their passports stamped.

Their paperwork processed, the Alliance team walks onto the tarmac to board the Thai Airline's plane.

July. They were yelling and making crude remarks while ripping up posters of the former president, placing all the blame on him for the current state of the city.

Kevin paused in front of the Sofitel Hotel, a once-beautiful edifice that stood in ruins before him. Two chairs and a carpet were piled on a cart in front of the building. Kevin recognized them as being from the restaurant where he and Joyce had celebrated their last wedding anniversary.

Those are probably the tail end of the treasures left in there, he assumed, turning toward the main post office. It appeared to be in good shape, though its doors were locked and chained shut.

"So much for picking up the mail!" he quipped.

Next, he headed toward the duplex where the Browns had lived and the Hotalen family had been staying. Tree limbs, broken furniture, books, papers and other debris cluttered the street. Glancing at some papers by his feet, Kevin recognized a weather-faded logo of The Christian and Missionary Alliance. He bent to pick it up. Ron Brown's name was on it. Looking more closely, he saw other mangled papers and books belonging to Ron and Myra.

His pulse quickened as he picked up a book and gently turned its ripped and weather-worn pages. He knew the book was beyond use, as were the others lying at his feet exposed to the wind and rain. But he also knew the message they contained was not limited to the paper and ink on which it was written.

Thank You, Father, he silently prayed. *Thank You that these lessons and their applications have been written on the hearts of young men and women who have been dispersed by this war and are now using what they have learned throughout the country.*

Dropping the book, Kevin walked through the open gate and stared at the duplex. His breath caught in his throat. Torn couch cushions were scattered on the porch, along with a clothes dryer, emptied of all its working parts. The doors and windows stood ajar, inviting someone—anyone—to enter and begin the mammoth job of cleaning up.

Picking his way through the rubble, Kevin felt sick. "What a violation of personal property!" he declared as he began to sift through the mess. Each room was strewn with at least eight inches of papers, books and broken household articles. The house had been stripped of sinks, toilet, lights, electrical outlets and anything else of value.

Ron's office was in total disarray, but a number of his books had been left behind. Kevin locked the doors and windows, hoping to deter further vandalism until he could come back and retrieve what remained.

Entering the kitchen, his eyes were met by a few recipe books and Tupperware® lids, and his nose was met by the foul smell of moldy spices that had been dumped on the counters and floor. Myra's red-handled mop lay in the middle of the room, crying out for someone to put it to use.

"Next time!" Kevin promised, as if it could understand.

Leaving the Browns' home, he headed for the other side of the duplex. Though the Hotalen family had been staying there, it was really the home of David and Tammy Noel who were on home assignment in the U.S.

Water poured from the front door. When thieves had helped themselves to the plumbing fixtures, they had left open water pipes behind.

I wonder where the main water valve is, Kevin asked himself, tramping into the soggy mess. He stepped over water-soaked photo albums and was grateful to find some pictures on a shelf, safe and dry. He put them in his pocket and continued his search.

Noise on the porch caught Kevin's attention.

"Oh no!" he cried, remembering his jacket and suitcase sitting outside. He splashed across the room and out the door, pursuing the thieves. His passport, money and camera were in his coat.

"Hey! Stop!" he yelled, running after them as fast as his tired legs would go. Scared, they dropped his things and ran.

Out of breath but thankful, Kevin reached

down and picked them up. He checked his
jacket pockets. Nothing was missing.

Haven't they stolen enough? he thought, shaking
his head and walking back down the garbage-
strewn street.

His next stop was Carol Erbst's apartment
where he witnessed a replay of what he'd seen
at the duplex. Everything was gone except
some scraps of paper and a few rotten grocer-
ies. Even the electric box had been torn from
its mounting on the wall.

Heavyhearted, Kevin resumed his tour of the
devastated city. It was like walking through a
ghost town. Destruction jumped out at him
from every direction. Even the cathedral on the
hill was missing its steeple.

Heading toward the Center, Kevin stopped
on the way at the residence of colleagues with
another Mission. He walked through the open
gates, past overgrown vines and pieces of broken furniture in the yard and yelled a greeting.
There was no response other than the echo of
his own voice.

Inside, everything was in ruins. Passing
through the kitchen, Kevin remembered deli-
cious meals and smiling faces around the table
that was no longer there. In the dining room
and office, documents were scattered over the
floor. A handful of unanswered letters sat on
the desk—the only intact piece of furniture
that remained. A family picture hung on the
wall. Kevin slowly reached for it. His fingers

gently wiped away the dust, and for several moments he stared at the photo, cherishing memories of his dear friends.

"Thank You, dear God, that they got out of here alive," he whispered, blinking tears from his light blue eyes.

Back outside under the hot African sun, Kevin quickly covered the few blocks to the Brazzaville Center for Christian Studies. His heart raced. *Dare I hope that it still stands?* he wondered.

Moment later, his eyes drank in the most wonderful sight they had ever seen. The Center stood!

The Nigerian Embassy, its neighbor to the east, was in bad shape, showing evidence of several rocket hits. Likewise, the International School to the west and the public school to the north bore the scars of battle. And the hospital just south of the Center had suffered severe bomb damage.

Kevin was amazed. "God must have plans for this place!" he joyfully declared as he opened the door. His amazement grew as he went from room to room. Not a thing was missing! Not a thing was damaged! Even the chairs were in their places around the tables. He stepped up to the podium at the front of a classroom and his mind's eye pictured the room full of students as it had been the last time he'd stood on that spot. He could almost see their expressions and hear their voices.

He carefully opened the attendance book and scanned the lists of names—names that belonged to young men and women who loved the Lord and were training to serve Him. How many of them had lost their lives in this war? Where were the others? How many had they led to Christ? He'd heard stories of some who had fled to their home villages and were spreading the gospel there, following the example of the believers in the early Church who were scattered from Jerusalem and preached the Word wherever they went (Acts 8:1-4).

Salty tears blurred his vision as he prayed for each one before closing the register and vacating the building.

Kevin talked to a soldier outside. "God has definitely had His hand on this place," he said, still elated by his discoveries.

"Yes," the soldier agreed. "It is God's house and He protected it. The military even used it as a fortress, but God didn't let them hurt it."

*   *   *

Kevin's joy soon turned to mourning as he entered his own family's home. Limbs from his daughters' dolls lay in the dirt by the front gate. Books and empty trunks cluttered the front porch. The kitchen door was missing. Walking through the door frame, Kevin entered the room in which his family had shared stories, laughs and tears over countless meals. A lonely bottle of soy sauce and a few tea bags sat among scraps of mildewed paper on the floor.

The scenes in the other rooms were reminiscent of all the houses he'd seen that day. Scattered books, broken shelves, everything of value gone. The master bedroom was in shambles. But one dresser drawer remained closed. Sliding it open, Kevin was relieved to find several valuable wood carvings right where they had been left.

His next stop was the neighbor's house. Mr. Ndinga, one of the few people still living in the neighborhood, was excited to see Kevin. And Larry, the Bellamys' poodle, affectionately licked his hand when he bent down to give the dog a pat.

"Do you know where Nicaise is?" Kevin inquired after a lengthy greeting.

"No," Mr. Ndinga answered. "I haven't seen him for over a month. I miss him. He was so courageous through the whole war. But he left here on October 13 and went south. It's a good thing he left when he did since the Cobras came that night. They probably would have killed him."

Kevin nodded. Being related to a colonel in President Lissouba's army would likely have meant death for Nicaise when Cobra forces took the city. At least now he knew that Nicaise had left town.

Mr. Ndinga went on to tell Kevin about the Cobra soldiers coming to loot the McCabe house. They made several trips, hauling load after load for four days. On the last day they loaded the parrot, cage and all, into the military truck and took the pet monkey as well. He was last seen hopping up and down on the roof of the truck as it drove away!

Kevin's last stop for the day was at the Bellamys' house. A rocket blast had left a gaping hole in the bedroom wall. Fire had destroyed what was left of the room. Other rooms suffered from water damage and mold. He found nothing salvageable.

Darkness fell shortly after Kevin had checked into the Bougainvillea Hotel, the only place in town that was functioning. He heard sporadic gunfire throughout the evening, telling him that it wasn't yet safe to bring his family back to this side of the river.

He opened his Bible to Psalm 49. "Do not be overawed when a man grows rich . . ." he read, "for he will take nothing with him when he dies" (49:16-17).

"Thank You, Lord, for that reminder," he prayed. "Please help me to remember that all we had belonged to You and You want us to store up treasures in heaven, not here on earth. And thank You, God, that You are good—all the time." Kevin closed his Bible and fell into a fitful sleep.

The next morning he walked to the beach. Once aboard the ferry, he rode back to Kinshasa lost in his own thoughts. He'd seen all he could take. And he was convinced that it wasn't yet time to move back to Brazzaville.

*   *   *

The Congo missionary team grieved the loss of their ministries and their possessions. They grieved for their hurting Congolese brothers and sisters. Why did God allow such atrocities? That question may forever remain unanswered. But believers are sure of one thing—God is in control. His plans are always perfect. What from one perspective looks like an interruption in the building of the Church in Congo may in fact be an acceleration. People who had no time for God when their businesses were flourishing and their possessions were accumulating have been struck with the harsh reality that these things can be instantly taken. And "What good is it for a man to gain the whole world, yet forfeit his soul?" (Mark 8:36). Through the loss of the temporal, people have been confronted with the eternal. And hundreds have met Jesus.

For a group of North American missionaries walking on the Congo road, the cost has been high. But each of them had made a commitment to follow God's leading down any road, at any cost. They have no regrets.

*   *   *

After six months of waiting, watching and seeking the Lord, the doors finally opened for the Congo missionary team to return. On February 23, 1998, Kevin and Joyce McCabe and Ruth Sterneman went back—but not to Brazzaville.

After evaluation, everyone including the American and Canadian regional directors for the Alliance in Africa, agreed that the capital city was not yet a safe place for missionaries to live. Pointe Noire, however, suffered only minor damage in the war and has become, for the time being at least, the new base for Alliance missions in Congo.

Part 2

The Cambodia Road

"You will not fear the
terror of night,
nor the arrow that flies by day,

. . . no harm will befall you,
no disaster will come near
your tent."

(Psalm 91:5, 10)

Map of Southeast Asia

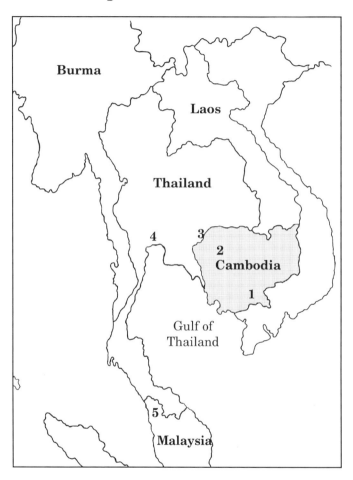

1. Phnom Penh
2. Battambang
3. Aranyaprathet (where the Battambang convoy crossed into Thailand)
4. Bangkok
5. Penang (home of Dalat School)

Map of Phnom Penh

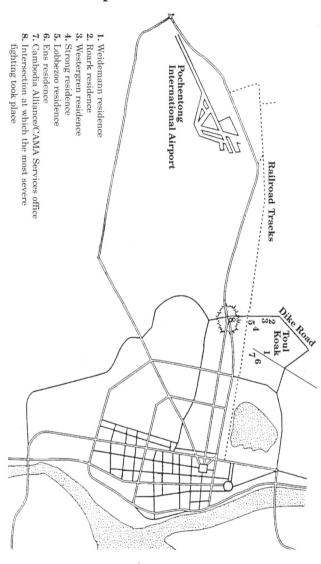

1. Weidemann residence
2. Roark residence
3. Westergren residence
4. Strong residence
5. Lobbezoo residence
6. Ens residence
7. Cambodia Alliance/CAMA Services office
8. Intersection at which the most severe fighting took place

Pochentong
International Airport

Railroad Tracks

Dike Road

Toul
Koak

The Cambodian Team

The Christian and Missionary Alliance
—Cambodia, July 1997

In Phnom Penh

Marie Ens

William and Ilana Lobbezoo
    Holly - age 2

Michael and Maureen Roark

David and Doris Strong

Donald and Esther Weidemann

Stephen and Mary Westergren
    Eric - age 8
    Kirsten - age 7
    Brent - age 2
    Kreg - age 10 months

In Battambang

Bounoeuy and Chanthan Kes
    Diana - age 5
    Sammy - age 2

David and Christine Manfred
    Joshua - age 8
    Joel - age 6
    Janelle - age 4

On Family Leave

Richard and Beth Drummond

On Home Assignment

Joyce Johns

Bounsoeuth and Syna Loa
 Justin - age 1

Paul and Teresa Masters
 Benjamin - age 12
 Caleb - age 10
 Jonathan - age 8
 Daniel - age 2

Timothy and Darlene Ratzloff
 Andrea - age 14
 Nicholas - age 12

David Rebok

Jeffrey and Heather Williams
 Liesl - age 7
 Linnea - age 6
 Jared - age 2

Chapter 9

Trouble in Town

Saturday, July 5, 1997

David Strong sat at the computer in the CAMA Services* office in Phnom Penh, Cambodia. *Whatever did we do without e-mail?* he wondered as he finished off a letter to his parents: "There have been a few noises in the city in the past week. So please continue to pray for things here. Nothing to get alarmed about, but just so you know—Cambodia hasn't arrived at complete peace yet."

Moments after he sent the letter, David heard an explosion. Jerked to attention, he sat upright in his chair, listening. Another explo-

---

*   CAMA Services is the relief arm of The Christian and Missionary Alliance.

sion echoed down the street, and then another, followed by distant gunfire.

David got up and walked out the front door.

"Did you hear those blasts?" he asked the Khmer (Cambodian) guard.

"Yes," the guard replied with a smile, his jet-black hair shining in the afternoon sun. "But they are far away."

David knew that "far away" to a Khmer can mean as close as two miles. He also knew that a 107mm rocket can travel a lot farther than that. He and the guard talked briefly, but the continued shelling "far away" made David anxious to be on his way home.

On the street, there was an unusual amount of activity. David wended his way through the crowds of people scurrying to and fro, many of them running. Motorbikes, Phnom Penh's most plentiful "taxis," buzzed past, their agitated passengers holding tightly to the seat's edge. David turned his vehicle onto the rutted dirt road that neatly divided the large market in half. Merchants were hastily packing up their jewelry, wares, fruits and vegetables. Something was definitely in the air.

David's mind turned back to that morning when he and his wife Doris had played tennis at the Olympic Stadium with their Australian friends. Before they left the courts shortly after 8 a.m., David had heard shelling in the distance, but wasn't alarmed—he'd heard it several times in the past month.

As the group walked toward their vehicle, they saw ten soldiers in army fatigues, carrying AK47s, M-16s and a B-40 rocket launcher.

"Maybe some big shot is in today's tennis tournament," David suggested, still not overly concerned by the familiar sight of soldiers.

However, before they left the stadium complex, they saw several other groups of soldiers, many of them heavily armed with chains of 50-caliber bullets draped in "Xs" over their chests and backs.

Maybe there was more going on at the stadium this morning than we realized, David thought as he bumped his way toward home. *Oh, God, please intervene,* he prayed. *Hasn't this little country been through enough?*

David was aware of Cambodia's history—a path marked by the footprints of war. Back in the 1800s, Cambodia had faced the threat of being swallowed by its stronger neighbors, Vietnam and Laos. Its government asked for help from France, at which point the small nation became a French protectorate.

In more recent history, Cambodia was not spared from involvement in the Vietnam War which spilled over its borders in 1969.

But nothing was so horrible as the war within—the regime of the Khmer Rouge led by the cruel tyrant, Pol Pot. Gaining power in 1975, he unleashed a holocaust that led to Cambodia's formidable reputation as the home of the "Killing Fields."

Hundreds of thousands of Cambodians were forced from their homes in Phnom Penh and fled to the surrounding countryside. Even patients were ousted from their hospital beds to join the hellish exodus. Many never made it out of the city, but died where they fell. Unspeakable horrors separated families and claimed 2 million lives. The government tolerated no criticism, dealing a deathblow to any who dared speak out.

Pol Pot and his ruthless collaborators set their sights on crushing the elite and the educated. People with money and/or possessions were targets, as were those with a fourth-grade education or higher. Anyone wearing eyeglasses—a sign of literacy—was added to the list of victims.

David and Doris Strong had visited the memorial sites and read of the multitudes brutally exterminated by a blow to the head from a club or a hoe. Others were buried alive, not considered worth even the cost of a bullet.

Mass graves became the final resting place for countless victims of the terror. The sunbaked bones of those who didn't receive the "honor" of such a burial lay strewn in the fields.

David shuddered as he brought his thoughts back to the present and pulled into the driveway of his temporary home. He was glad to see his wife waiting to greet him at the door. (They were living for two months in the home of Tim and Darlene Ratzloff who were on a summer furlough.)

Once inside, David glanced at the table with nine places set.

"Looks great!" he said, "but I wonder if our company is going to make it." David and Doris were expecting their field director Don Weidemann and his wife Esther for dinner, as well as colleagues from Hong Kong, Joseph and Liza Ng, with their three children. The shelling was getting closer. It was sounding like a good day to stay at home. But it was only 4 p.m.—things could calm down before their guests were expected.

David and Doris went into the living room and sat down. Doris opened her Bible to Psalm 91. "You will not fear the terror of night, nor the arrow that flies by day, . . . no harm will befall you, no disaster will come near your tent" (91:5, 10), she read aloud.

"There's a promise we can hold onto," David said thoughtfully.

The gunfire outside was increasing in volume. Seldom more than five minutes passed without the noise of flying bullets filling the air.

Like most Alliance workers in Phnom Penh, the Strongs had neither a telephone nor a two-way radio.

"I wish we had a phone," Doris told her husband. "We could call the Weidemanns and the Ngs and tell them not to come."

David nodded his agreement. They would just have to wait and see what happened.

*   *   *

Quite accustomed to war sounds in the distance, Steve and Mary Westergren thought
nothing of what they heard that Saturday
morning. Their cook returned from the market
around 10 o'clock reporting that there were a
lot of soldiers on Dike Road behind their
house. Steve called the U.S. Embassy; no
warnings or reports had been posted, so the
Westergrens went ahead with the plans they
had made for their day off.

Shortly after noon, leaving their youngest
child, ten-month-old Kreg, with a Khmer baby-
sitter, the Westergren family joined their As-
semblies of God missionary neighbors for an
afternoon of swimming at the International
School of Phnom Penh. Both families were
completely oblivious to any trouble in the city.

While they played in the pool with their children, they heard booms in the distance. Looking west toward Toul Koak, the neighborhood
in which they lived, they saw dark clouds in the
sky and concluded the noise was simply thunder.

About the middle of the afternoon there was
a close, loud boom.

"That's not thunder!" all four adults exclaimed, nearly in unison. Now very aware that
the city was being shelled, they hurriedly gathered the dripping children and piled them into
their cars.

On the streets, people were running this way and that, closing up shops and scurrying to their homes. The smell of gunpowder was strong in the air.

The Westergrens had not gone far when they passed a friend's house.

"You'll never get back to Toul Koak now," he warned. "Stay here."

"No way!" Mary declared impatiently. "My baby is in Toul Koak."

The streets were emptying quickly as the Westergrens drove toward their home. They later heard that others were unable to get into Toul Koak, but they made it without incident.

*   *   *

A few blocks away, first-term missionaries Bill and Ilana Lobbezoo were preparing to go to their language tutor's house for a party, while two-year-old Holly took her afternoon nap. They had made a trip to the market earlier in the day and had seen soldiers, weapons and rocket launchers lining the streets as they went. The political uneasiness in the city over the past few weeks made such things almost normal.

But at the market things weren't normal. Some of the shops were closed. Tension filled the air.

"Something is up," Bill commented, glancing toward his wife. "But that's life in Cambodia!"

While Holly slept that afternoon, the sounds of gunshots and mortar fire erupted just blocks from the Lobbezoos' home. Bill and Ilana looked at each other, surprise and concern crossing their faces.

"Whatever it is, it will probably be a temporary problem," Bill said optimistically. "I hope!" he added with a slight smile.

"I hope so too," Ilana agreed.

An hour passed and the fighting got heavier. The Lobbezoos decided that this was a good night to stay home. The party would have to wait for another day.

*   *   *

It was Saturday afternoon. Marie Ens had invited her friends and coworkers Kim Eng and Sakhon to her home for a prayer meeting.

Both women looked worried as they climbed the steps to her second-floor apartment. They had seen an unusual number of soldiers on their way to her house—and tanks as well. They were convinced the situation was bad.

Marie welcomed them into her bright living room and offered them seats on colorfully cushioned wicker chairs. Before they could begin to pray, their conversation was interrupted with the loud boom of a missile. The prayer meeting ended before it started, and the women hurried for their homes.

The instructions to the Alliance team in Phnom Penh, should such a situation arise, were to stay home. As the explosions and shooting continued, Marie conversed with Yoko and Sho, the Japanese couple living in the apartment below hers. They were in Cambodia with Overseas Missionary Fellowship (OMF). Yoko was on her way out the door to buy bread when the fighting started. She decided not to go. That gave Marie something to do to take her mind off what now seemed like an impending crisis. She went back upstairs and busied herself mixing up a batch of bread big enough to share with her neighbors. They, in turn, shared their fruit and yogurt with her.

*　　*　　*

In the same Phnom Penh neighborhood, Mike and Maureen Roark were awakened by distant artillery fire early Saturday morning. It was becoming a familiar sound since they had moved into their new home. The Roarks had been in Phnom Penh for only ten months after having spent fifteen years in Indonesia. The Indonesian government, without explanation, had refused to renew their visas. So they had been reassigned to Cambodia.

For most of their time in Indonesia, Mike and Maureen had been the most isolated missionaries on the Alliance team, living in a remote village of 1,400 people in the jungles of

West Kalimantan. It was a difficult transition for them to adapt to the urban noise and pollution, not to mention the endless crowds—the million people with whom they shared the ancient, temple-dotted city of Phnom Penh. Indonesia and Cambodia are both in Asia, but that is where the similarities end.

There were other things that shocked their senses. They hadn't yet gotten used to the sight of beggars lined up at storefronts along the dusty roads, struggling to keep body and soul together. Many of them limped along on rickety crutches, having lost a leg to one of the millions of land mines buried under Cambodia's bright green rice fields. Even though "de-miners" have been hired by the government and different aid agencies to find, dig up and destroy the land mines, the job is immense. Frequent accidents continue to kill and maim hundreds of innocent victims. Perhaps the Roarks never would be accustomed to the sight of these helpless souls begging for a measly twenty cents with which to buy a bowl of noodles from a street vendor.

Having studied Cambodia's history and visited the memorial markers at the "Killing Fields," Mike and Maureen were beginning to understand the fears that strangled the hearts of these war-weary people. And so the sounds of fighting that roused them from their sleep that Saturday morning in July 1997 sent shivers up and down their spines.

About 11 o'clock there was a lull in the fire. Maybe the trouble was passing. But then it erupted again—louder and closer. Things in their house began to shake with each blast.

Maureen walked into the kitchen where their house girl was preparing a meal. Her wide eyes held Maureen's.

"This reminds me of the Pol Pot days," she said, her mind overflowing with memories of the horrible atrocities that had forever contaminated Cambodia's history. "I pray it doesn't happen all over again. But I have Jesus with me now, so I'm not afraid."

Concerned about the siblings who were under the girl's care, Maureen decided to send her home.

Mike and Maureen had no idea of the severity of the situation. Had they known that their landlord, a cabinet minister who lived below them, had been whisked away to a safe place early that morning, they may have understood that this wasn't just a passing skirmish.

They spent the evening in the dark, with no electricity, wondering what might happen next.

*   *   *

Saturday morning for Don and Esther Weidemann had been spent at the graduation ceremony for the Phnom Penh Bible School where Don, as field chairman, had been invited to give the commencement address. In true

Asian fashion, the program was long with countless speakers and presentations.

Though seasoned missionaries, having spent two years in Vietnam and over twenty-two in Hong Kong, the Weidemanns had been in Cambodia less than a year and had not yet gained a command of the Khmer language. Unable to understand much of what was being said, Esther sat through the ceremony that morning, her mind wandering to a conversation she had with her house helper shortly before they left.

Owen had appeared at the door early. After bowing her head and raising her hands together in front of her face in the customary Cambodian greeting, she told Esther she would not be coming to work that day. Esther understood that much, but was unable to determine Owen's reason. She knew it wasn't that she was sick, nor that anyone had died, yet she could tell that Owen was upset.

I wonder what it was she was trying to tell me, Esther mused as yet another speaker came to the podium and began his speech. She knew Owen's husband was a soldier. *Perhaps they know something the rest of us don't,* she speculated.

At last the ceremony ended and, after a quick stop at Lucky Burgers (Phnom Penh's answer to McDonald's®), the Weidemanns were on their way home.

At 3 o'clock that afternoon the sounds of shelling could once again be heard. The Weide-

manns could tell it was in Toul Koak—the
neighborhood in which they and all their missionary colleagues lived.

The phone rang. It was Joseph Ng.

"Do you hear what we hear?" he asked.

"Yes, I'm afraid we do," Don replied.

"Are you still planning to go to the Strongs'
place tonight? Or do you think it might be wise
if we all stayed home?"

Don had already made up his mind.

"We're not going anywhere. Let's stay home.
With all this racket, I doubt the Strongs will be
expecting us anyway." It did feel strange
though, not to show up to a meal they had
been invited to. But they knew David and
Doris would understand.

A short while later the phone rang again. It
was the U.S. Embassy, wanting to know what
was happening in Toul Koak. Don reported
what he had seen and heard. The embassy replied by warning him that there would likely be
more significant action to come.

"There's an ammunition dump near you," the
American voice said. "If it gets hit, there could
be major destruction. We advise you to stay
downstairs if you can. Stay away from windows
and don't go anywhere."

Since Don had been designated as the warden for the U.S. citizens in that area—namely,
the Alliance Mission team—he was asked to
share this information with those for whom he
was responsible.

"Great!" Don exclaimed as he replaced the receiver. "We're not allowed to leave the house and I have this information I'm supposed to communicate to a bunch of people who have no phones!"

Esther shared his frustration. Only one other missionary family—Steve and Mary Westergren—had a telephone. All they could do was pray together for the safety of their teammates. One thought that eased their minds was that there were a lot fewer people to be concerned about than there had been a few months earlier. The Alliance missionary team in Cambodia had reached a peak of fifty-eight North Americans (thirty-one adults and twenty-seven children) during the first few months of 1997. But a couple of families had left Cambodia permanently, and others were out of the country for vacation or home assignment, leaving only twenty-five—sixteen in Phnom Penh and nine in Battambang, nearly 200 miles northwest of the capital.

As darkness fell on the troubled city, the sounds of war faded into silence. In homes throughout Toul Koak, missionaries hoped and prayed that the peaceful sounds of the night meant an end to the fighting. Only in the morning light would they know for sure.

Chapter 10

"The Longest Day of Our Lives"

Sunday, July 6, 1997

Morning came all too soon and with it the bone-chilling sounds of war. Don and Esther Weidemann were wakened at 5:30 a.m. by a thunderous roar that shook their house.

"So much for hoping this was over last night," Don moaned, rubbing his eyes. He got up, looked out on the deserted street and prayed for the city he had so quickly grown to love.

While Don was in the shower, Esther heard someone at the front gate. She hurried out and was shocked to see Sambo and Tuan, both of whom worked at the Alliance office. They had come by motorbike. Why had they made this dangerous journey? Had someone been injured or killed?

"Why are you here?" she inquired.

"We want to make sure you are all right. Do you need anything?"

Esther felt tears well up in her eyes. These men had come at considerable risk to their own lives just to check on their safety.

"We're fine," she assured them. "There's nothing we need. Thank you for coming, but please, go home and try to stay safe."

Throughout the morning the fighting got heavier and closer.

"This place is going to get hit soon," Esther exclaimed between explosions.

Don nodded.

"Let's get on the floor—with pillows over our heads."

They had hardly gotten settled when there was a knock at the door. It was their landlord, who lived on the same property.

"May our children take shelter in your house?" he asked, fear evident in his dark eyes.

Don and Esther were not sure their house was any safer than the others, but they welcomed the young people in. From their window they could see black smoke billowing high into the sky between them and the airport about five miles away.

"A gas station has been hit," the landlord explained as he left.

Esther was more scared than she ever remembered being. She looked at her husband.

The expression on his ashen face told her something was drastically wrong.

"What is it?" she asked.

"I don't feel well," he replied as he lowered himself to the floor. The pain in his abdomen was severe.

Esther hurried to the medicine cabinet while Don lay writhing on the floor. *I wonder if it's his appendix? Or maybe a kidney stone? Or maybe—I hope—just gas pain from all the stress?*

Kneeling beside him, she administered Tylenol®, TUMS® and prayer.

"Oh, God, please touch him," she said. It wasn't even noon yet and Esther felt like she'd been up a whole day. When would it end?

*   *   *

Marie Ens also woke early Sunday morning to the sounds of war. It wasn't long until she too had company. Her former house helper Rame, along with her husband and four children, arrived at her door.

"May we stay with you?" Rame asked after Marie responded to their greeting. Rame's pleasant face was creased with fear. "The shelling is very heavy by our house," she explained, motioning in the direction of the loudest noise.

"Yes, of course," Marie said, welcoming them in with a smile. She was glad for the company—something to take her mind off of the incessant noise. She went to her barrels of sup-

plies and pulled out some toys to occupy
Rame's children. While they played, the adults'
eyes followed the columns of black smoke rising into the southern sky.

"It's coming from over near our house,"
Rame lamented. "There's probably nothing
left."

Marie longed to comfort Rame, to take the
fear from her heart. They prayed together, ask-
ing God to intervene in this nightmare that was
becoming ever more personalized.

While Marie and her guests listened to the
sounds of battle, her missionary colleagues
only a five-minute drive away were experiencing more than just the sounds.

*   *   *

Firing tanks on the road a block away from
their home jarred Mike and Maureen Roark
from their sleep that Sunday morning. They
went to the window. People were streaming
into a nearby vacant building, eyes wide with
bewilderment.

"I suppose their homes have been destroyed,"
Mike concluded. "They have nowhere else to
go."

From the windows of their second-floor
apartment, Mike and Maureen had a clear line
of vision across their neighbors' property to
Dike Road, now the front line of the battle.
They watched as three small wooden houses on

the road took a direct hit from a rocket, instantly reducing them to gray clouds of smoke and ash.

"How many other homes has that happened to?" Maureen wondered aloud, her heart and mind traumatized at the sight.

"That wind is not going to help any," Mike added, watching the billows of smoke being herded across the sky by the strong gusts. "It's blowing the fire in our direction."

Lord, I know all that we have belongs to You, Maureen prayed silently, fearing the fire might eventually reach their house. *So now I want to let go again of our home and all that's in it. If You want to take it away, that's OK. It's Yours.*

A blast from a nearby tank caused Mike and Maureen to jump. The windows and the china rattled.

"Let's get away from the window." Mike took Maureen's hand and led her into the kitchen. They stood there for a moment, contemplating where the safest place would be. The bathroom. That would put more cement walls between them and the fighting than any of their other rooms would.

Another blast rocked the house. This time plaster rained down from the ceilings and the curtains were sucked against the windows.

Mike reached for the radio and tuned in to Voice of America, trying desperately to pick up any news of events in Phnom Penh. He also tried the BBC, flipping back and forth between stations trying to get any information he could. He turned the volume to maximum and still they were unable to hear the newscast above the roar of rocket fire and machine guns surrounding them.

*   *   *

Bill and Ilana Lobbezoo were sure that the blasts which jarred them from their sleep would do the same to Holly. But their two-year-old daughter continued to sleep while the house shook with incoming and outgoing mortar fire. Even when the power went off, taking with it the familiar whir of the overhead fan, Holly didn't stir.

"Thank You, Lord, for closing her ears to this noise," Bill whispered as he looked in on the little girl. Miraculously she slept through until the power was restored later in the morning.

By that time, Bill and Ilana were almost accustomed to hearing explosions every few minutes and were able to keep themselves from cringing. Staying on the floor and away from windows, they played with Holly and listened to the BBC broadcast from London. Having been in Cambodia only a little over a year, Bill and Ilana still lacked the language skills to understand the political terminology on Khmer news reports. Nor did they have a telephone to contact any of their colleagues, so the BBC was their sole source of information.

Gradually they began to piece the story together. Since 1994, Cambodia had had two co-prime ministers who had formed a coalition government. But neither leader was content to share the office. In fact, they hated each other intensely. On July 5, 1997, second prime minister Hun Sen deposed first prime minister Prince Ranariddh. As the Lobbezoos began to comprehend what was happening, they realized that the whole Alliance missionary team in Phnom Penh lived in the same neighborhood as several military and cabinet men on Prince Ranariddh's side. In fact, one of his generals lived just around the corner from their house.

Not unexpectedly, the general's house became one of the targets for Hun Sen's forces. That explained the increasing noise outside. Bill decided to play a Christian video. Animated figures led them in songs of praise, providing a blessed distraction from the battle raging nearby. Holly happily bellowed out her favorite Sunday school songs for the neighbors and soldiers to hear.

*   *   *

Over breakfast Sunday morning, the Westergren family talked about the shelling they heard in the distance. It was closer than it had been Saturday night, but there was no sense of urgency around the table.

"Let's go up on the roof and see if we can tell what's going on," Steve suggested to eight-year-old Eric, the oldest of his four children.

Eric happily raced his father to the rooftop.

"Wow! Look over there, Dad!" he exclaimed pointing toward the airport.

Steve looked in the direction of his son's wide-eyed gaze. Flames were leaping into the sky beneath clouds of thick, black smoke.

"Looks like a gas station got blown up," was Steve's best guess. "Let's go tell Mom."

The neighbors, missionaries from another Mission, were also outside, debating whether or not to leave Toul Koak. As they talked back and forth over the fence, Mary spotted another fire directly to the south.

"This is getting too close for comfort," she told her husband. Steve and Mary hurried their family inside. The neighbors decided to flee their home, though the Westergrens later heard that they ended up stuck in Toul Koak anyway.

Steve and Mary both knew that the number one rule was to stay put in the midst of shelling. It would be foolish to try to relocate to a safer place. Anyway, where was there a safer place? In this confusion, it was anybody's guess. They chose to take cover in Steve's office since it had no outside windows and faced away from the street.

At 9:30 a.m. the fighting broke loose, and the five longest and most frightening hours of the

Westergrens' lives began. During lulls in the fighting they sat and sang choruses and prayed. During the worst of it they laid flat on the floor. Some of the explosions were so close that the whole house shook. In addition to the sounds of heavy weapons, they could hear bullets bouncing off the metal fence in their yard. Steve and Mary held their children close, sharing in their fear. How long would this go on?

*   *   *

"Here we go again," David Strong moaned when he and Doris were awakened by gunfire at the first sign of daylight.

"Do you think we should pack a bag in case we have to leave?" Doris quizzed her husband.

"That's probably a good idea," he agreed, "especially since no one could call and warn us they're coming."

They carefully stowed their laptop computer into one carry-on bag, along with two small wedding pictures and as many clothes as would fit. More clothing and other necessities filled the other bag. Then David came up with a plan to set out three extra sets of clothes each—if they had to leave quickly they would dress in layers and thus have more than just one clean shirt! By 6:10 a.m., their bags and extra clothes were waiting by the door.

By 7 o'clock, streams of refugees were beginning to make their way past the Strongs' house.

Some were pulling carts stocked with their meager belongings. Others carried bundles on their heads. They were coming from Dike Road, less than half a mile away.

There was a knock on the door. It was Mr. Hein, their landlord, with his wife and two children.

"Please come in," David said, with a smile.

"Yes, we all want to come into your house," Mrs. Hein said.

As the shelling got closer, David and Doris sought out the safest room in the house for them and their company. The bathroom was surrounded by its own four walls plus the outer walls of the house. Taking the cushions from the living room furniture, they lined the bathroom floor. At 9 o'clock, while the Hein family chose to stay in the kitchen, the Strongs settled into their newly designed, wall-to-wall-cushioned "bathroom bunker" to listen to the BBC news.

"Heavy fighting has resumed this morning in Phnom Penh . . ."

"No kidding!" David commented sarcastically.

" . . . and the international airport has remained closed since yesterday afternoon."

"I guess that means we're not going anywhere," Doris concluded.

After the news, David stuck his head around the corner to check on the Heins.

"Come join us," they said.

David and Doris both felt the bathroom would be safer but, wanting to stay together with their friends, they brought some cushions and joined them in the stairwell beside the kitchen.

Explosions continued to rip through the neighborhood with deafening consistency.

"Incoming!" someone shouted after the house shook with a boom.

"Outgoing!" someone else called out a few moments later. Six scared people huddled on the kitchen floor under cushions, guessing the direction of each shell.

"Outgoing? Incoming? I can't tell anymore," Mrs. Hein laughed nervously during a moment of quiet.

Holding tightly to her cushion, Doris remembered the words she had read in the Psalms the previous afternoon. "You will not fear the terror of night, nor the arrow that flies by day, . . . no harm will befall you, no disaster will come near your tent" (91:5, 10).

"These aren't exactly 'arrows flying by day,' but they're close enough! And, like the psalmist, we can trust God to protect our 'tent.' " David and Doris assured each other of God's protection.

Doris looked at her watch. "I sure wish this day would hurry up and pass," she said with a sigh. "It's only 10:30 and I feel like I've already lived a full day."

*   *   *

Around 1 p.m., there was a lull in the fighting. Keeping well below the level of the windows, Maureen Roark scooted into the kitchen to prepare lunch.

"Since all the soldiers seem to be stopping for lunch, I think this might be a good time to run and check on the Westergrens," Mike said, following her into the kitchen. They had been concerned for Steve and Mary and their children who lived only five houses away and thus were also very close to the front lines.

"Maybe they've been in touch with Don and Esther," Maureen added. Aside from the Weidemanns, the Westergrens were the only Alliance missionaries in Phnom Penh with a telephone.

Mike walked out onto the street and looked around. Not a soul was in sight. He walked quietly past four houses to the end of the street. Rounding the corner across from the Westergren house, he looked toward an intersection 200 feet away. An armored personnel carrier with a machine gun mounted in front was parked there. Slowing his pace, he walked calmly across the street, hoping not to draw attention to himself. Then, keeping close to the neighbor's brick wall, he approached the Westergrens' front gate and let himself in.

"What are *you* doing here?" Steve exclaimed in surprise.

Happy to be together and find out that everyone was OK, they began to exchange stories.

"Have you managed to get through to Don and Esther?" Mike wanted to know.

"Yes, we've talked to them a couple times. They're hearing it too, but are farther from the action than we are. They told us we're welcome to go to their house if we can get out of here."

"That sounds like a wise idea to me," Mike counseled, looking at Steve and Mary's four wide-eyed youngsters. "You need to get to a safe place as soon as you can."

Five minutes into their conversation, the fighting started again with great intensity and everyone was back on the floor in Steve's office. Loud machine-gun and tank fire cut their conversation short.

Suddenly it began to rain.

"Now's my chance to run for home before Maureen gets too worried," Mike decided. The firing had begun so soon after he left home that Maureen could easily have thought he was caught in it. After a quick good-bye, he disappeared down the street. *Thank You, Lord, for this heavy rain,* he prayed running up the stairs to his home, grateful that even the fighting broke for meals and rain!

Heavier fighting picked up again a short while later when the rain died down.

"We might have to get out of here this afternoon," Maureen thought aloud.

Mike nodded, noting the mixture of sadness and disappointment in his wife's voice.

Maureen began to pack a bag in case of evacuation. What to put in it? She changed her mind a few times, evaluating what meant the most to her. Taking a break, she looked out the window.

"Look at this," she called to Mike.

A group of Prince Ranariddh's soldiers were climbing over the six-foot brick, barbed-wire-and-broken-glass barrier below their bedroom. They obviously didn't know they were entering the yard of a cabinet minister in Hun Sen's government.

The soldiers had just finished streaming into the Roarks' yard when the Westergren family stopped on the street. They had decided it was time to risk the five-minute drive to the Weidemanns' house.

"Are you OK?" Steve shouted from the driver's seat.

With a group of soldiers under the window, Maureen wasn't sure how to answer.

"Yes, we'll be fine," she yelled back. "We're going to stay here for now."

The Westergrens drove away, leaving Mike and Maureen to watch the nervous soldiers carry on discussions in their yard. They noticed their landlord's bodyguard was in the group, his face betraying the severity of the situation. When the defecting soldiers asked who lived in the house, the guard told them it was the home of Americans. If he had let on who his boss was, it could have cost him his life. He chose to use the Roarks as a shield.

One soldier moved toward the street and looked carefully in both directions. He turned and said something to the others who began shedding their camouflage jackets and changing into civilian clothes.

One of the defecting soldiers collected weapons from the others and placed them in the covered sewer on the other side of the road from the Roarks' house—six AK47s, a machine gun, hand grenades and camouflage vests filled with ammunition. Then, one by one, they walked through the Roarks' gate and blended into civilian life.

*   *   *

During the five minutes from their home to Don and Esther Weidemanns' house, the Westergren family felt like they were playing with death! They had barely pulled out of their driveway when they were alarmed to see a tank sitting only three houses away. A soldier perched on top of it waved at them furiously. Ignoring him, Steve carefully guided their vehicle down back roads so as not to become a target for a stray bullet. Soldiers were hiding out in trees. Others waved them on as though they were half crazy.

It seemed like a lot more than five minutes

had passed by the time they arrived safely at Don and Esther's house.

"I'm so glad you made it," Esther said, giving Mary a welcoming hug.

Mary looked frazzled. Five harrowing hours in Steve's office with an eight-year-old, a seven-year-old, a two-year-old and a baby had been almost more than she could handle.

"Come in and make yourselves at home," Don said warmly, having recovered from his bout with pain earlier in the day. He now felt well, but the concern etched on his face revealed the load of responsibility he carried for his colleagues spread throughout Toul Koak.

Steve and Mary were relieved to have their family away from the worst of the onslaught. They could still hear shelling, but it was not nearly as loud. And they were free to walk around the house and play games to keep the children's minds off the noise outside.

As darkness once again crept over the city, the fighting subsided. The electricity had been off for hours. Everything was very dark—and quiet. Exhausted, the Weidemanns and their guests settled down for the night, grateful to be alive and grateful that they knew at least some of their team was OK.

*   *   *

During the lunchtime break in the fighting outside, the Strongs and their landlord's family raised themselves from the kitchen floor and had lunch. Mr. and Mrs. Hein both had portable telephones with them. David made repeated attempts to contact Don and Esther, but with no success.

A game of Yahtzee® with the Hein children helped to pass the time after lunch—until a shell exploded thirty feet from their house, causing everyone to jump. Leaving the game where it lay, the families reclaimed their positions on the floor, pulling pillows over their heads.

Another shell exploded, this time in the front yard, accompanied by the sound of crashing glass. Minutes later they heard more glass breaking upstairs.

No one spoke. But a million thoughts raced through each mind.

I can't believe I've brought my wife into this mess! David thought. *What have I done?* His mind rewound to the previous week when he and Doris had celebrated their first wedding anniversary. His memory replayed the serenity of their time beside the pool of a nearby retreat center. What a contrast to the current cacophony of falling shells and rockets.

"Are you OK?" he whispered to Doris.

Her response was a quiet and confident, "Yes, I'm OK."

A brief afternoon downpour brought a temporary lull in the fighting. Borrowing Mr. Hein's telephone, David tried again to reach

Don and Esther. He dialed the number and listened to the phone ring.

"Hello?" Don's voice came over the line.

"Hello, Don. This is David . . ."

"Hello?" Don repeated.

"Don, this is David. Can you hear me?"

"Hello? . . . It must be someone with the wrong number."

"No, Don, it's me, David. . . ." He heard Don hang up the receiver. The rain slowed and the fighting commenced.

The minutes ticked by and the group on the Strongs' kitchen floor wondered what was happening. With machine-gun fire coming from the front of the house, they knew soldiers were on the road.

At 4:45, Mr. Hein's phone rang. His friend informed him that three of Prince Ranariddh's generals and their men had surrendered to Hun Sen's forces. They had one more general to capture—and he was in Toul Koak. That explained the severe fighting going on around them.

Two long hours later the shelling finally slowed. The sounds were reduced to sporadic blasts of machine-gun fire retreating into the distance. With gratitude for the quiet, the group lit candles and shared a meal together. When bedtime came, they moved the dining room table into the kitchen. David and Doris made a bed of cushions under it. The Heins settled into the living room.

"I am so glad this day is finally over," Doris whispered, stretching out on their makeshift bed.

"Likewise," David replied. "I'm sure it was the longest day of our lives."

They slept like babies.

* * *

It was late Sunday afternoon. As the fighting simmered down for the day, Mike and Maureen Roark stood on their balcony overlooking the street and watched the silent procession of neighbors pass by, their scanty possessions bundled on their heads. Unkempt children, ragged clothes hanging from their thin bodies, plodded beside their parents. The fear on their faces couldn't be hidden.

"What are you thinking?" Maureen asked, probing Mike's thoughts.

"It reminds me of the pictures I've seen of people leaving Phnom Penh when Pol Pot came in 1975. It's eerie. And it makes me angry. This war is just so crazy—and it's the common people who are suffering. I feel more anger than fear," he added, trying to put his feelings into words. "How about you?"

"I feel very calm," Maureen answered, reflecting on the events of the day. "I guess it's just a sense that God is with us—and that's all that really matters."

Darkness closed in and the street became

very still—more still than either of them had ever seen it. A chorus of crickets and frogs filled the evening air. Enjoying the tranquillity of their dark balcony, the Roarks finished their day with a cup of tea by candlelight.

Chapter 11

Meanwhile in Battambang

July 5-7, 1997

"**B**attambang is quiet," David Manfred told his wife Chris Monday morning. "The town is tense, but there is no fighting yet. I'm glad you and the kids are safely out of here though," he added, grateful that his family was across the border in Thailand.

David and Chris Manfred and their colleagues Bounoeuy and Chanthan Kes were the only North American missionaries in all of Northwest Cambodia. They made their home in Battambang, a city of about 100,000 people, nearly 200 miles northwest of Phnom Penh (which translates into a bumpy seven-hour ride).

Immediately after he hung up the phone, David received an urgent call on his U.N.

walkie-talkie. It was a warning to stay away from the provincial governor's house. Ten seconds later: *Boom!* A rocket-propelled grenade exploded into a government leader's home only half a mile away.

"It's started! Let's get out of here!" urged Bounoeuy Kes, David's Khmer-American missionary colleague.

David ran to his motorcycle and started the engine. Bounoeuy hopped on behind him and they took off. Another explosion roared from the same direction as the first.

As David and Bounoeuy raced toward the main bridge in Battambang they noticed soldiers on the far side setting up a machine gun on a tripod. The only way to the Manfreds' house was to cross that bridge.

"Go, go, go!" Bounoeuy yelled in David's ear.

And that's exactly what they did. As they flew past the soldiers, both men ducked below the machine gun's potential line of fire. The soldiers were still busy setting up the gun and the missionaries passed without incident.

Moments later the little motorcycle turned onto the Manfreds' street. David was thankful to see that their house helper had opened the gate and the front door. Frightened, David drove the motorcycle straight through both and into the house!

*   *   *

On Friday evening, July 4, David and Chris had heard on a BBC shortwave broadcast that Cambodia's two prime ministers had suddenly decided to leave the country. This was not a good sign, but they assumed the departure of the leaders was due to one of the frequent skirmishes between their "bodyguards." (Before the coup, both prime ministers referred to their soldiers as "bodyguards" in an effort to conceal the fact that they each had a small army.)

David and Bounoeuy had planned to leave the following morning for a weekend of ministry in Pursat, three hours south of Battambang, along with two Cambodian pastors and John Bromley, a young man from Canada on a short-term summer missions trip. After checking in at the United Nations' office and hearing that all was clear, they decided to proceed with their trip.

They arrived in Pursat late that morning and spent the rest of the day visiting the three new churches in the area. As they drove over the dirt path to one of the churches they were greeted by about twenty children wearing crowns made from gold paper. They had been waiting three hours for the men to arrive! It was the first time the people of that congregation had seen missionaries and they wanted to welcome them properly.

The team from Battambang had an encouraging day of ministry. They spent the night in the home of a pastor in Pursat. With his eleven children plus guests, there were more than twenty people sleeping in a 20′ x 30′ house.

The next morning Bounoeuy preached at one of the churches. Following the service, they shared lunch with the congregation and then piled into the Land Rover to return home. David turned on the 12 o'clock BBC news on the vehicle's shortwave radio. The lead story was that there was heavy fighting between the two political parties in Phnom Penh.

"This is serious!" David exclaimed. "We've got to get going—now!"

As David guided the vehicle over the torturous road, Bounoeuy gazed out the window, thoughts racing, and prayed for his beloved homeland. He dreaded the thought of more war. There'd been too much already. He remembered the fear among his family and friends when the communists came to power. He remembered overhearing late-night discussions in which his father and stepmother, in hushed tones, made plans to flee Cambodia. He remembered the hot July day in 1979 when his family managed to escape across the Thai border and find shelter in a refugee camp.

Please, Lord, don't let the atrocities of those years be repeated, he prayed silently, watching the mighty trees of the jungle forest blur together as they sped by.

Bounoeuy had always had an appreciation for the towering hardwoods of Cambodia's forests.

As a young boy he had watched his father fell trees on their remote farm to clear land for his crops. Fascinated by the huge trunks and leafy foiliage, Bounoeuy wondered how they came to be. He asked his father, but got no answer. He asked the Buddhist monks, but again was not satisfied with the response. Buddhism is silent on the question of creation.

Bounoeuy had never heard of Jesus Christ until he was in Thailand. His stepmother met up with a friend of her brother in the refugee camp. This friend and fellow refugee was an Alliance pastor who introduced Bounoeuy's stepmother to the Lord. Before long his father, three sisters and brother also became believers in Jesus.

To be Cambodian is to be Buddhist, a bitter and rebellious Bounoeuy reasoned. *How can my family betray their Cambodian identity and embrace this foreign religion?*

Life in the refugee camp was boring for eighteen-year-old Bounoeuy. One day for something to do he agreed to accompany his family to a church service. Sitting on a hard, uncomfortable bench in a hot and dusty meeting place, he paid little attention until the sermon began. The pastor's topic that morning was creation! For the first time in his life, a desperate young Bounoeuy heard about the Creator God. Several days and countless questions later, he was finally convinced of his need for God and asked Jesus to be his Savior.

In 1981, Bounoeuy arrived in the U.S. with no money and only one change of worn clothes. Eleven years later he returned to Cambodia as a missionary to his own people, endeavoring to introduce them to the Creator God he met in a refugee camp.

"Look at that!" David Manfred exclaimed, pulling Bounoeuy from his reverie. David was pointing to large guns mounted on tripods at the edge of the road—guns that had been covered the day before. Trouble was definitely brewing.

*   *   *

Meanwhile in Battambang, it was business as usual in the Manfred and Kes households. Unable to get to church because David had their vehicle, Chris stayed home with their three children—Joshua (eight), Joel (six) and Janelle (four). She invited Chanthan Kes to bring her children over as well, allowing Chanthan time to prepare for her daughter Diana's fifth birthday party planned for that afternoon when David and Bounoeuy got home.

Around 11:30 Chris had a visitor. A representative from the international community came to inform her of a security meeting that was to take place a few minutes later. In light of the fighting in Phnom Penh, which could soon begin in Battambang as well, the meeting was scheduled to discuss evacuation to Thailand. Since Chris had children, she was told to prepare to leave.

She ran upstairs and spent the next ten minutes in a whirlwind of packing. She handed each of her children a backpack filled with clothes and instructed them to add their favorite toys.

There was another knock at the door. It was Johannes, a good friend from the international community. He had come to report on the outcome of the meeting.

"It was decided at the meeting that all the expats are leaving in a convoy at 1 o'clock," he said somewhat matter-of-factly.

One o'clock! Chris thought, looking at her watch. *We are supposed to be out of here in an hour?*

"Are you going?" she inquired of Johannes.

"Yes." The tone of his voice told Chris that the situation was serious.

"OK, we're ready," she heard herself say. But her mind was full of doubts. *I don't want to leave like this. There's no closure, no time to say goodbye. And what about David and Bounoeuy? Can't we wait until they get home?*

With preparations complete for her daughter's birthday party, Chanthan, still unaware of mounting trouble, returned to Chris' house to pick up Diana and two-year-old Sammy. Not wanting the children to hear the urgency in her voice, Chris pulled her aside and filled her in on the events of the morning. When Chanthan

heard the latest developments, she quickly
went back to her house to pack for her family.

In the meantime, Chris tried to call Don and
Esther Weidemann in Phnom Penh to tell
them what was happening and ask for their advice. In spite of her repeated attempts, she had
no success.

Chris scribbled a quick note for David and
then she and Chanthan informed some of their
Cambodian workers of the change in plans.
Loading their belongings and their children
into the Kes' car, Chris and Chanthan drove to
the U.N. office to join up with the convoy.

It seemed so strange to be leaving. There
were no signs of unrest in the city—it appeared
to be a regular day. Chris' heart was sad and a
few tears brimmed her eyes as she drove. *Am I
looking at this city for the last time?* she wondered.

The two women stood in line at the U.N.
building to record their car and all the passengers in it. Still not convinced that it was necessary for them to leave, she turned to a Khmer
guard standing nearby.

"What do you think?" Chris asked him. "Do
we really need to leave?"

The guard looked away, avoiding the question.

Chris and Chanthan talked about going home
and waiting for their husbands whom they expected would return in a couple hours. Then
they could leave together if they needed to.

"I don't think that's a good idea, ladies," a voice behind them said. It was Colonel Mead, an Australian military advisor to the Cambodian army. He had overheard their discussion. "The road to Pursat is closed," he continued, "so the chance is small that your husbands will get back to Battambang today."

"They've traveled on closed roads before," Chris protested. "They know how to do it. I know they are coming. We'll catch up to the convoy when they get here."

"Your husbands will be happier knowing you have left and are safe," the colonel reasoned. Finally convinced, the women nodded their assent.

Chris and Chanthan crowded into the car with their five children. Feeling less than confident about guiding the vehicle over rutted roads and makeshift bridges, Chris gratefully accepted an offer to drive from John, an English worker with Lutheran World Service.

With John at the wheel, they took their place in line. As they meandered through the streets of Battambang, Chris and Chanthan looked for signs of trouble. But they saw none. The local traffic seemed normal. People were smiling and relaxed.

"I'm still not so sure it's really necessary to leave," Chris commented. But the decision had already been made—they were on their way.

Chris wanted to keep the mood light for the sake of the five children in their car. Yet she didn't want them to be unaware of what was happening.

"Do you know what we're doing and why?" she asked.

"Yes," six-year-old Joel explained, "we're evaporating."

"That's close," his mother responded with a chuckle. "We're evacuating. Do you know what that means?"

Joel's wise older brother answered.

"It means were being vacuumed out of Cambodia." So much for the seriousness of the moment!

As they bumped along the torturous road toward the Thai border, Diana Kes wondered when she was going to get her birthday cake. The answer was, "We'll see what we can do." The fifteen-vehicle convoy stopped for a break a short while later. Taking a brief walk around the parking lot, Chris mentioned Diana's question to her German friend Uta who was riding in another car. Uta went back to her car, plucked out a piece of fresh homemade cake and handed it to the little girl.

"This isn't birthday cake," Diana objected. "It doesn't have any candles! There should be five candles on it!" It tasted good nevertheless.

As the convoy closed the gap between itself and the Thai border, the expatriates saw more and more soldiers. The men in uniform weren't standing around in the usual relaxed manner of Khmer soldiers, but appeared nervous and alert to sounds and movement around them. Rounding another corner, the convoy was waved down by a group of armed men.

Chanthan surveyed their faces as they walked the length of the cars.

"These soldiers are frightening," she told Chris, her usual calm demeanor shattering. "These guys have a reputation of being rough. They extort more money from travelers than any others. They can get pretty violent at times."

Chris looked out at the soldiers. Most of them appeared to be less than eighteen years old, but trying desperately to be tough in order to gain respect. Every time one of them strolled past the car, Chanthan cringed. Fortunately their car stood out from the rest. The Manfreds and the Keses were the only expats in Battambang with children—it was the only one with little white kids. When Joel and Janelle smiled at the boy soldiers, even the toughest of them softened and returned the smile.

While they waited, someone got out of one of the cars ahead of them and began taking pictures. Nervous soldiers confiscated the camera. "No one is to take any pictures," they ordered sternly.

An hour later, the convoy was permitted to continue. Six long hours after leaving Battambang they arrived at the Thai border. The communal sigh of relief was almost audible.

Thai officials met them and directed them to

park their cars in neat little rows off to one side. As Chris and Chanthan and the children got out of the car, they were descended upon by reporters. They felt like their every move was being photographed and videotaped.

Not knowing what to do with this group of people at an illegal border crossing, the Thai guards had them form two long lines. Chris watched with amusement as these poor men tried to figure out the proper protocol. She couldn't help but feel sorry for them in their polyester uniforms that were a few sizes too small and an unfortunate shade of brown.

As darkness enveloped the group, the Thai informed them they were free to go to a designated hotel. Once more they piled into their cars and, after being stopped by more reporters who wanted to know every detail, headed for the hotel.

Having never been to Thailand, Chris was amazed at how drastic a difference crossing a bridge from one country to the next could make. There were street lights, traffic signs and paved roads with curbs. What a contrast to the garbage-strewn, rutted roadways of Cambodia. There was even a 7-11®!

Chanthan kept the kids together while Chris arranged for rooms and unloaded the car. While she was at the hotel desk, the telephone rang. It was for her. *Who could possibly know I'm here?* she wondered, taking the receiver.

"Hello?"

"Hello, Chris. This is Boyd Hannold calling from Bangkok." Boyd, the field director for the Alliance in Thailand, had seen them on television and called to see how they were doing and if there was anything he and his staff could do to help. It was very encouraging for Chris to be able to rehearse the experiences of the day and to request prayer for David and Bounoeuy since they didn't know where they were. Boyd also asked about the rest of the Cambodia team, but Chris was unable to tell him anything. She too wondered about her teammates in Phnom Penh. Were they even alive?

Chris and her children finally got settled in their room. It didn't take Janelle long to discover they had a bathtub. (Their house in Cambodia had only a shower.) The boys instantly felt the need to test the "bounceability" of the beds. Unlike their wooden beds covered with foam in Battambang, beds with mattresses and springs were great fun!

It was 10:30 and the kids were still wired. Chris turned on the television.

"Look, we're famous!" Josh exclaimed as their picture flashed across the screen. There was several minutes' worth of footage of the convoy. Unfortunately they were unable to understand a word of what was being said, so they still didn't know what was happening in Cambodia.

After the news, Chris tried to get the kids to sleep. They prayed together before turning out the light.

"When will we see Daddy again?" Josh asked after praying for all the missionaries still in Cambodia. Chris didn't quite know how to answer that question and others like it.

"Soon, we hope," she finally responded.

It was after midnight when the children finally fell asleep. But Chris tossed and turned, her mind filled with questions. *Where is David? Did they get trapped in Pursat? Did fighting break out? Is he safe? When will we see him again?* In the wee hours of the morning a sense of God's peace seemed to cover her like a blanket. She fell into an exhausted sleep.

At 7:30, while the children were still sleeping, there was a soft knock on the door. It was Chanthan.

"If you would like to talk to your husband, he's on the phone in my room."

Chris was so relieved to hear David's voice. The good news was that he would be arriving in another convoy later that day.

"Battambang is quiet," he reported. "The town is pretty tense, but there are no signs of action. I'm glad you and the kids are safely out of here though."

Chris and Chanthan spent a peaceful day at the hotel, awaiting the arrival of their husbands.

*   *   *

David, Bounoeuy and the others had an uneventful trip home from Pursat. There was very little traffic, but the heavy guns that had been covered the day before were now ready for use. There was no time to waste. David skillfully guided the Land Rover around potholes and over ruts with record speed.

Arriving in Battambang at 2:40, they stopped for gas and were told there had not as yet been any fighting in town. Nearing home, they were waved down by a friend who explained that the majority of expatriates, including all the women and children, had already been evacuated.

David's heart sank. Praying that the Lord would help him think straight, he went to the U.N. office to find out what they knew. Yes, his wife and children, as well as Bounoeuy's wife and children, had gone in the convoy to Thailand earlier that day. He also found out that another convoy was planned for the following afternoon and that he and Bounoeuy could join it. Apparently the top generals in Battambang from both political parties did not want to fight, but they would if they received orders from Phnom Penh to do so. It was a "wait and see" game now.

Returning home, David began to pack.

I wonder if I'll ever see this place again, he thought as he opened drawers and selected only what would fit in his suitcase. Deep down he expected he'd be back, and yet he had nagging doubts. It was a sad night.

Monday morning, David and Bounoeuy were at a local telephone shop where they found out where their wives and children were staying and placed a call to the Thai hotel. How good it was to talk with them and to find out that they really were safe and comfortable.

Explosions rang out minutes later. David was glad he had been able to tell Chris truthfully that it was quiet in Battambang so she would not be overly worried. After the two initial explosions, peace reigned again—at least on the surface.

The Battambang U.N. security committee called an emergency meeting for later that morning. Recent reports had been received that there was fighting north of Battambang on the road to Thailand. The U.N. was now recommending that the convoy not leave that afternoon. Reluctantly, David and Bounoeuy accepted the news, even though it meant not being reunited with their families. After all, they were now at the mercy of the officials. It would be the height of stupidity to try it on their own.

As the meeting was breaking up, Colonel Mead strolled through the door.

"Good news, folks!" he announced in his Australian accent. "They'll let one more convoy through."

Colonel Mead had led the first convoy of expatriates to Thailand the afternoon before and had returned via some very insecure areas for the next run. Normally Mead was stationed in Phnom Penh, but he just "happened" to be in Battambang when the fighting broke out. Because of his position as military advisor, he knew all the major players from both political parties. The two warring factions had given him assurances that they would delay their war until after the expatriates passed—if they left Battambang by 1 o'clock that afternoon.

"I have a feeling that Battambang is going to be a war zone within the next twenty-four to seventy-two hours," the colonel speculated grimly. "We'd better evacuate as many as we can today. Things are really volatile out there. This could well be our last opportunity to get a convoy out of here."

David, Bounoeuy and John Bromley were at the U.N. office at the appointed time.

"Travel slow and stay together," Colonel Mead instructed. "If we are stopped, do exactly what the soldiers tell you to do. And if shooting should start while the convoy is stopped, get out of your car and lie down in the ditch next to the road. Do not run!"

The nine vehicles with forty-one expatriates wound their way slowly toward Thailand. T-54 tanks marked the front line, their tracks carved through the mud beside the road, heading into the cover of the brush. Soldiers could be seen crouching behind dikes bordering the rice paddies. Two miles further on stood another line of soldiers—the opposition—ready for battle.

But, as promised, the weapons remained quiet and the convoy passed without incident.

*   *   *

Daylight gave way to darkness as Chris Manfred and Chanthan Kes again watched themselves on the Thai evening news.

"If the convoy really did leave this morning as it was supposed to, they should have been here by now," Chris observed, a note of dejection in her voice. Chanthan nodded.

"I guess they're not coming today. Hopefully tomorrow . . ." her voice trailed off.

Leaving Chanthan's room, where they had been watching out the window in anticipation, Chris took her children to get ready for bed. They had just prayed together when there was a loud knock on the door.

"They're here! They're here!" Chanthan cried excitedly.

Moments later David and Bounoeuy were smothered in hugs from their wives and children.

Chapter 12

When Elephants Fight

Monday, July 7, 1997

As the early morning sun began to rise over Phnom Penh, Esther Weidemann pulled herself up through clouds of sleep. It took her only a moment to realize that she had not been rudely awakened by firing guns and exploding mortars. All was quiet—quieter than usual for a Monday morning.

Does this mean it's over? she wondered.

Others shared her optimism. Over breakfast with the Westergren family, they shared a cautious hope that the volatile situation had ended and peace had returned.

Then, distant shots rang out. Everyone was

still, listening for more, dreading a continu-
ation of the previous day's battle. But thankfully they heard only silence.

"What do you think, Steve?" Don asked.
"Should we venture out to check on the others?" Both couples were concerned for their
colleagues spread around Toul Koak. As the
field director, Don especially felt the responsibility to make sure all had survived the weekend. There was really no way to know how the
others were except by paying them a visit.

"Yeah, I think we should," Steve agreed, sharing Don's sense of concern.

Their first stop would be at Mike and
Maureen Roark's place. The devastation that
met their gaze as they drove down Dike Road
was unbelievable. A burned-out tank stood as a
silent witness to the defeat of Prince
Ranariddh's men. Rows of small homes were
laid waste, pile upon pile of charred rubble.
They were relieved to find Mike and Maureen
unhurt, their home undamaged.

After Don and Steve's visit, Mike and
Maureen ventured out to call on a few of their
friends. They went first to visit their language
tutor. Having survived the horrors of the Pol
Pot regime, she was terrified to leave her
home. The weekend fighting had recalled terrible memories for her, memories of losing many
in her family. With them came renewed fear.

Not hearing any gunfire, Mike and Maureen
then decided to drive the short distance to

their house helper's home. Over 100 small thatch, wood and cardboard houses in her neighborhood had been completely wiped out. As they walked past the burned ruins, Rachinee came running out to meet them. The fire had swept along the block, but did not jump the empty lot just two doors down from her house. Thankfully, it was still standing.

Rachinee hugged Maureen tightly and both women started to cry, thanking God for His protection.

Rachinee introduced Mike and Maureen to her neighbors. They had lost everything. Out of the ashes of their home they pulled a small wooden platform for Maureen to use as a chair. Her heart ached as she shared in their sorrow. All they had left were the threadbare clothes on their backs and the faded rubber thongs on their feet. Surrounded by such appalling grief and devastation, Maureen felt like she was right where God wanted her to be.

The Roarks were quiet on the drive home, each lost in thought. The events of the hours just past had made a powerful impact. They felt gratitude for their own protection intermingled with anger toward the army and pain for those who had lost so much.

Back in the house, Maureen slowly emptied the bag she had begun to pack the day before. She did not want to leave. Her mind rewound to their arrival in Cambodia in September

1996, less than a year earlier. They had come with broken, disconnected hearts, grieving for the Indonesian friends they had left behind. The thought of learning a new language and culture was overwhelming.

Now, ten months later, they realized that God had done a miraculous work in their hearts. He had given them a deep love for the gentle Cambodian people. The thought of a possible evacuation produced a similar wrenching in their hearts that they felt leaving Indonesia. They wanted to be here, in the midst of Phnom Penh's agony, to comfort their new friends.

*   *   *

Don and Steve made their way from the Roarks' house to see David and Doris Strong. Don felt his pulse quicken as they rounded the corner and saw the broken limbs of a mango tree littering their yard. Looking at the house, he noticed shattered windows and glass all over the front porch.

Hearing the sound of a motor and footsteps on the walk, David and Doris ran around from the back of the house to meet them. After being assured that the Strongs were unhurt, Don and Steve stayed only a few minutes before continuing on their rounds.

David and Doris decided to stay home for the day. Sporadic bursts of gunfire convinced them that they didn't want to go far. They did spend some time though surveying their yard, thanking the Lord for protecting them when the fighting had been so close—literally on their doorstep. Their mango tree had taken the brunt of one of the explosions they had heard, tearing off several of its branches. Charred splinters of wood littered the ground under the tree. Bright white spots on the trunk beckoned passersby to look where bullets had torn away the bark.

Pieces of shrapnel mixed with the broken glass were strewn over the Strongs' front porch. There was even a piece of shrapnel inside a pair of shoes that had been sitting by the door. And eight window panes had fallen victim to the flying shards of metal. Assessing the damage more closely, David noticed bullet holes in the upstairs windows. Two of them had penetrated the glass, but the mosquito screen just inside the glass was neither torn nor indented in any way. The bullet heads were nowhere to be found. Miraculously the shots had not entered the house.

"Amazing!" David said softly, shaking his head. Then he remembered the verses from Psalm 91 that he and Doris had read two days earlier. "God really did protect us from 'the arrow that flies by day' didn't He? And no disaster came to our 'tent'!"

People were milling around on the road, greeting neighbors and exchanging stories. An uneasiness came over the crowd as they saw soldiers approaching. Scurrying back into their yards, they watched as fifty uniformed men marched past single file, each with a red ribbon tied around his arm, signifying his allegiance to Hun Sen, the communist leader who had apparently been successful in overthrowing Prince Ranariddh.

*   *   *

Marie Ens was very glad to see Don and Steve. She was fine, she said, though concerned for those who had suffered such great losses.

Marie's friend Rame and her family were still with her. Rame was anxious to check on her home. She was afraid that it would be nothing but ashes. Filled with apprehension, she left her family at Marie's place and made her way through her mostly ruined neighborhood. A firestorm had raged down the street, leaving only a few charred posts and twisted tin roofs behind. Over 100 houses were nothing but rubble. Miraculously, the flames stopped before they reached Rame's house.

Within a short time, she rejoined her family back at Marie's house, praising the Lord that their home had been spared. And yet tears fell as she told of their friends and neighbors who had lost everything—victims of their government's war.

*   *   *

Don and Steve had one stop yet to make—
Bill and Ilana Lobbezoo's place.

Within a few blocks of the house, they saw a
large number of soldiers marching down the
street. As they got closer, they came to a roadblock and were not allowed to pass. They were
told that Hun Sen's soldiers were headed for a
home occupied by one of Prince Ranariddh's
generals. They were going to arrest him.

Knowing that the general lived just a few
doors from Bill and Ilana, they prayed for a
peaceful arrest and for Bill and Ilana's safety,
then headed the vehicle toward home.

Driving back to the Weidemanns' house,
Don and Steve noticed that Hun Sen's soldiers
had gone shopping—looting homes and trash-
ing businesses. Pedicabs were loaded down
with refrigerators, televisions, motorbikes—
anything moveable that was of value. Soldiers
were running helter-skelter through the city,
stopping people at random, demanding their
money and gold and shooting those who didn't
have enough to satisfy them.

The *Phnom Penh Post* reminded its readers of
a Khmer saying: "When the elephants fight,
only the ants die."[1]

The elephants had fought. As Cambodia's
leadership battled each other for control, the
country's poor suffered most. Hundreds of
people who had few material possessions be-

fore the war were now left completely bereft of even the basics of life. No one knows for sure how many were injured or lost their lives. One source reported fifty-eight dead and over 200 wounded, ninety-five percent of whom were civilians.[2]

There were more reports of looting. People who had fled to safety in other neighborhoods during the fighting returned on Monday and Tuesday. Some were stopped at gunpoint and forced to wait while soldiers completed the job of ransacking their homes.

Other soldiers, red ribbons waving from their uniforms, broke into shops and markets, followed by civilians who took what little they left behind. Armored personnel carriers and other military vehicles were piled high with what the soldiers considered the spoils of their victory.

Several gas stations were closed because their pumps had been blown up in the battle. It was an opportunity for bold, entrepreneuring soldiers to go into "business," taking money from civilians in exchange for siphoning gas into their tanks from the station's reservoirs.[3]

*   *   *

With the power still off and the fans not running, it was hot in Bill and Ilana Lobbezoo's house that Monday afternoon. Yet two-year-old Holly lay down for her nap and slept soundly.

Bill and Ilana had decided to stay inside for another day until they were sure it was safe to leave. While Holly slept there was a knock at the door. It was their landlord stopping to see if they were OK.

A few minutes later, Don and Esther Weidemann arrived, reporting that the roadblocks were no longer in place and the rest of the Alliance team were all fine. It was safe to go out.

After the Weidemanns left, the Lobbezoos decided to make a quick trip to buy more fuel for their generator. Telltale signs of battle were obvious throughout the neighborhood—sandbags, tank tracks on the pavement, shot-off treetops and burned-down shacks.

They met up with Khmer friends and their hearts ached for these people whose memories of terrible times in the past had been reawakened.

"The fighting is not over," their friends warned sadly. "What's ahead will be worse than what has just passed."

Endnotes

[1] Jason Roberts, "Khmer Sayings," *Phnom Penh Post*, July 12-24, 1997, p. 11.

[2] "Death Toll," *Phnom Penh Post*, July 12-24, 1997, p. 3.

[3] "The War's Over—Let's Go Shopping," *Phnom Penh Post*, July 12-24, 1997, p. 5.

Chapter 13

"Pull Us Out of This Mess!"

July 8-9, 1997

Phnom Penh was uncomfortably quiet Tuesday morning. The market was not yet up and running. Though a few merchants were open for business, most of the city looked like a ghost town.

Looting continued as soldiers and civilians helped themselves to other people's belongings. Bicycles moved down the streets, laden with stolen stereos, televisions and other household items. Several car and motorcycle dealerships were completely emptied of their stock. One reported losing over 1,000 motorcycles!

The airport remained closed to commercial flights. Looters cleaned out the silent terminal, emptying duty-free stores of their merchandise, stripping lounges of doors, furniture and air conditioners, and even taking the luggage X-ray machines.

Grieving people sorted through the rubble that remained of their homes. Marie Ens saw the door of opportunity wide open and ran through it.

Accompanied by Cambodian helpers, she drove to the Olympic Market. It was closed, the merchants afraid the soldiers would help themselves to their goods and their money. Someone directed Marie to a small street market where she was able to purchase sleeping mats, rice, fish, pots, dishes and spoons.

Returning to the burned-out sections of Toul Koak, Marie and her helpers began sharing the love of Jesus by distributing their purchases to over 100 families who lacked the essentials for survival.

*   *   *

David and Doris Strong drove down Dike Road, less than a mile from the home in which they were staying. Electric wires lay haphazardly around the remains of burned houses. To their left was the shell of a charred tank. At the next intersection another ruined tank gave mute testimony to the weekend's chaos. They stopped to watch as people dismantled it, hoping to sell their scavenged treasures as scrap metal.

While the Strongs were out, they saw an airplane circling the city. It went around three times before landing.

"I guess he's checking out what shape the runway is in," David observed.

They found out later the plane was from Thailand, the first of three flights for the evacuation of Thai citizens.

"I wonder if the U.S. Embassy has any evacuation plans." Doris mused.

"I don't know," David replied. "Let's go check it out."

At the embassy they were told that the Thai evacuation had been planned for several days and that it was not a result of the immediate situation. They were also informed that there were no plans for evacuation of American citizens.

The missionary team had thought about evacuating. Now the decision was made for them—there were no flights leaving the country.

Rumors abounded. There was talk of civil war.

Maybe this is just a lull in the storm, Don Weidemann reasoned. *Maybe it's our window of opportunity to get out of here.*

He called a meeting of the missionary staff the following morning to decide what they should do.

*   *   *

Nine o'clock Wednesday morning found the eleven adults and five children of the Alliance team in Phnom Penh at Steve and Mary Westergren's home. Their mood was solemn. Several of them didn't even want to think about the possibility of evacuation.

They prayed and they talked. On one side of the discussion were the indications that peace had apparently returned to Phnom Penh and that the doors were wide open for ministry. How could they leave when so many hurting people had so many pressing needs?

On the other side were the persistent rumors of impending civil war. If they were dead or seriously injured, they wouldn't be able to have a ministry anyway. Plus they had already been through a traumatic few days. Perhaps it would be best for the health of all of them to leave the country for a few weeks to regroup.

As the discussion continued there was a knock at the door. It was Yung Sot, the president of the Cambodian Alliance Church.

Steve Westergren exchanged a knowing glance with his wife. The chances of him showing up had been slim since he had been at their house just the day before. Steve and Mary had prayed that God would send Yung Sot back to offer counsel to the missionaries.

"How would you feel if the missionaries all left for a few weeks?" Don asked him after they had prayed together.

"I would be sad," he said, the emotion

showing in his deep brown eyes. "But it is all right."

The group continued their discussion. Don asked if anyone had read anything from Scripture during those few days that spoke to the decision before them.

David Strong read from Psalm 80:19. " 'Restore us, O LORD God Almighty . . . that we may be saved.' I feel a need for restoration," he continued. "Maybe God wants to bring that about by temporarily removing us from this country."

In her heart, Marie Ens wanted to stay. She had faced evacuation from Cambodia before— only there was no discussing the matter that time. She and her late husband Norman had been among the group of North American missionaries ordered to leave the country with four days notice at the beginning of the Pol Pot regime in 1975. Nearly twenty years passed before Cambodia once again opened her doors to missionaries other than those with relief agencies. Marie, now a widow, moved back to Cambodia in 1994.

And now she sat in a meeting where they were discussing leaving again. She desperately wanted to hear the Holy Spirit whisper, "Stay!" But she too had only the conviction that she should leave.

Leaving Cambodia was the last thing that Mike and Maureen Roark wanted to do. But God spoke to them through the words of the prophet Amos. "But the LORD took me from tending the flock . . ." (7:15). They reluctantly agreed that they thought God was directing them to leave.

Finally, Don read Psalm 79:9 from *The Message*. In that contemporary version, the verse reads, "You're famous for helping; God, give us a break. Your reputation is on the line. Pull us out of this mess!"

The group was in agreement. Even though they did not want to leave, they believed God was leading them to do so. Don made the final decision. They would attempt to leave the country.

Making the decision was one thing—actually getting out was quite another. Leaving the meeting, Don and Esther decided first to see if they could get some help from the U.S. Embassy. The help amounted to a bulletin board with the phone numbers of commercial airlines—none of which were flying! They also had the name of a charter service that was making several flights daily to Bangkok.

The next stop was the travel agent responsible for the charter service. They were already fully booked for Wednesday, they said, but there was a chance for a Thursday flight if they got to the office early the next morning.

David and Doris Strong received word that Don had been unable to obtain tickets. A couple hours later they decided to make a trip to the embassy to see if any more information was available or if an evacuation was in the works.

Behind the embassy building were two big tourist buses with large American flags hanging from them. "I bet they're planning an evacuation after all," David concluded as he drove past.

Inside the embassy, David and Doris were told that there were no plans for evacuation. But they were given a sheet of paper with the address of the travel agent who was selling tickets for charter flights to Bangkok.

"Some of our coworkers went there this morning," David explained, "and they couldn't get tickets."

"If there is a demand," the lady behind the glass responded, "they will continue to arrange flights and sell tickets."

Feeling bold, David asked another question.

"What are the two buses with American flags behind the embassy for?"

"Oh . . . umm . . . they are for a body we are trying to get back to the States. A tourist was killed last week and with the airport being closed for several days, we've been unable to ship it out."

"You need two buses to carry a body?!"

At that point, a man stuck his head out from around a corner.

"We are using the van back there for the body," he explained. "As far as the buses are concerned, anybody in this country can put any flag from any country on any bus. Those are not our buses."

"So there is no plan for evacuation?" David pressed.

"That is correct," the man responded, disappearing as quickly as he had appeared.

The Strongs decided to go to the travel agent who was supposedly selling tickets. It wasn't hard to find. The building was swarming with people. They wrestled their way inside through a rude and noisy crowd, all desperate for tickets.

"Are you selling tickets for tomorrow's flight to Bangkok?" David asked when they finally reached the front of the line.

"Yes."

"Even for sixteen people?"

"Yes. Just be here tomorrow morning by 7:30 and you will be able to get the tickets."

On the way home, the Strongs delivered the message about the availability of the tickets. It looked like they were all going to be leaving after all.

*   *   *

Somewhere in the middle of all the running around, Don and Esther received a call from their oldest son Brian. The news was that their youngest son Fred and his wife Sharon had just had their first baby, a girl named Esther Grace.

"Little Esther's birth is being robbed of the attention it deserves," Grandma Esther told

Don when she hung up the phone. "*She* should be in the limelight, not us." Her grandmother's heart wanted more than anything to be there with her family and to hold her tiny namesake.

Chapter 14

"Will God
Leave Too?"

Thursday, July 10, 1997

Don and Esther were up early Thursday morning and, after a quick breakfast, made their way to Transpeed Travel. A growing number of people was crowding around the entryway to the small office.

Although the establishment was open for business, the doors were closed and securely locked. In an effort to keep the crowd orderly, the man in charge allowed only a few hopeful travelers to enter at a time. As customers finished their business he unlocked the door so they could leave. Each time one person left, several others pressed toward the door to take his or her place. The office manager made several fruitless attempts to have the crowd form an orderly line. Exasperated, he finally gave up.

Additional office workers arrived. As each one entered the building, the crowd took advantage of the opportunity to push and shove. But at least with a larger staff on duty, there was hope the "line" would move faster.

"There are plenty of seats available," the office manager yelled, attempting once again to bring some order to the group. "There are five flights to Bangkok scheduled for today, each with 300 passengers. We will keep adding flights as long as there is a demand. Please be patient!"

*   *   *

David and Doris Strong listened to the 6 o'clock "East Asia Today" news on the BBC. Among the top stories was a report that forty Americans from the U.S. Embassy staff in Phnom Penh were being evacuated.

"That explains the buses!" David quipped.

The news about Cambodia was not good. It only served to assure the Strongs that leaving the country was a wise decision.

At 6:30 there were guests at their gate. It was Mrs. Sakada and Chantha, their contacts from the orphanage where they had been filling in while the Ratzloffs were on summer furlough. Both had recently become Christians.

"Are you really going to leave?" Mrs. Sakada asked sadly.

"Yes," David responded, "but we are planning to come back in a few weeks."

"If you leave," she continued, "does that mean God will leave also?"

David and Doris spent the next hour explaining to Mrs. Sakada and Chantha that God was staying in Cambodia and He would be with them wherever they went, no matter what happened.

*   *   *

Don and Esther waited for at least an hour in the increasing crush of people before they gained admittance to the office. Once inside, the wait was far from over, but at least there was air-conditioning—and much less pushing and shoving. Only three clerks were issuing tickets and each transaction seemed to take a very long time.

While the line crept forward, Don and Esther discussed their plan for departure.

"It would be a lot easier to get everyone to the airport if we went on two separate flights," Don concluded.

They watched people coming and going for a few more minutes and learned that tickets were being sold for only one flight at a time. As each flight was filled, they moved on to the next. By the time the Weidemanns got to the counter, tickets were being sold for the flight at 1:45 that afternoon.

"What do you think?" Don asked his wife. "Should we get all sixteen tickets now? Or should we get some now and some later?"

"Do you want to go through this push-and-shove routine again?" Esther reasoned.

That settled it. They would get tickets for everyone now.

As with everything in Cambodia, the tickets had to be paid for in cash. At $280 each, the grand total was nearly $5,000. With only $20 bills in his satchel, Don counted out and handed over a big pile of money.

Tickets in hand, he and Esther headed back to Toul Koak to announce the departure time to their colleagues. Each was allowed only one carry-on bag. The news was met with various reactions—some relief, some panic, some dismay.

Their next stop was the CAMA Services office. Esther ran in to tell the Cambodian staff that they had the tickets and that Don would be back in a few minutes to take care of business.

"Today?" they replied in chorus, looks of shock and disbelief on their faces.

Esther nodded, "Yes, today—at 1:45." Tears blurred her vision as she got back into the truck and headed toward home.

With less than two hours in which to be ready to leave, there was a flurry of activity. Marie Ens was in the middle of distributing food and other essentials to the poor when she received news of the departure. She turned the funds over to her Cambodian helpers, quickly packed and said tearful good-byes to the people she loved so dearly.

Aware of the continued looting, Mike and Maureen Roark left their home and vehicle as secure as possible, while at the same time trying to prepare themselves for the possibility of never seeing them again. But much harder than letting go of their things was bidding farewell to Rachinee and others whom they had grown to love.

One of the Cambodian CAMA staff drove the Weidemanns' truck, loaded with missionaries and baggage, making two trips to Pochentong International Airport. The fifteen-minute ride past demolished homes and ransacked businesses brought tears to the sober group, each deep in his or her private thoughts.

Only privileged vehicles were allowed to drive right up to the airport, so the missionaries piled out with their baggage at the main entrance and walked in. They immediately saw that the airport terminal, riddled with bullet holes and totally looted, was in no shape to be used. The control tower was also damaged, but apparently in working order. *I sure hope so, anyway!* Esther thought, staring at the bullet-pocked structure.

All passengers were directed to a covered area next to the terminal. The Alliance team joined the crowd they estimated to be in excess of 1,000 people, waiting to have their tickets processed. Makeshift tables were set up under a concrete structure that thankfully provided a bit of shade. A gentle breeze and a light rain eventually brought welcome relief from the heat.

There were three steps each passenger had to take before heading out onto the tarmac, none of which were organized in any way. First, each one was required to produce the receipt from his or her ticket in order to obtain a boarding pass. Then they were required to pay the usual $15 per person airport tax.

"Is that some kind of a cruel joke or what?" Don exclaimed.

"Really!" Mike agreed. "After the government troops shoot the place up, they charge us to *not* use the facilities."

There was no choice. They paid the tax.

Lastly, they went through an immigration check to have exit visas stamped in their passports. Finally cleared, they trudged out onto the tarmac and to the waiting aircraft.

The Alliance team gathered near the back of the line waiting to board. The deafening roar of the plane's engines prohibited conversation. No one was in the mood for visiting anyway. The flow of passengers climbing the stairs into the rear of the plane was stopped twice by airline personnel who were counting heads at the door.

Maybe there aren't enough seats, Mike Roark thought hopefully. He and Maureen did *not* want to leave. Giving God one last chance to keep them in Cambodia, they stepped out of their place in line and moved to the very end. Others stared at them questioningly, obviously incredulous that anyone would not want to escape the chaos and fear of the city. For a few moments it looked like their wish to stay may be granted. But the line moved again and they found themselves following their teammates up the metal stairway into the belly of the plane. Mike swallowed hard as he stole one last glance at the city.

Even though they were the last passengers to board and there were no seating assignments on the plane, Mike and Maureen had seats together. "I guess God really wants us on this plane," Mike conceded, buckling his seat belt.

With every seat full, the door was closed and the plane taxied down the runway. Esther Weidemann expected to feel great relief as they lifted off. But instead, a deep sadness flooded her heart. Tears ran down her face.

* * *

The Kes and Manfred families stayed for three days in the hotel just across the Thai-Cambodia border. They listened for news of what was happening in Cambodia, but received very little. One moment the news was hopeful, the next it was discouraging. They nicknamed their place of lodging the "Flying Rumors Hotel."

Leaving their vehicles in a nearby garage on July 10, the expatriate refugees from Battambang chartered a bus to take them to Bangkok. While in the immigration office getting official Thai visas in their passports, the missionaries were amazed to meet one of the CAMA Services staff from Thailand who had somehow found out about their arrival and was waiting to help with anything they might need. She also escorted them to the Alliance Guest Home, which was no small feat in Bangkok traffic, where the painted lines on the roads are taken as mere suggestions and are rarely followed!

The Battambang missionaries were made very welcome at their home-away-from-home in Bangkok. Not long after they were settled in their rooms, the rest of the Cambodia team arrived, having just flown in from Phnom Penh. The whole team was now safely together. What stories they had to share! And questions. When would they return to Cambodia? Would they ever be able to return at all? Right now, all that was sure was that God had carried them safely away from the war. What the future held, only He knew.

Chapter 15

God Is Building His Church

July 11- August 11, 1997

R elieved to be removed from the threat of further fighting, the Cambodia team devoured any news coming from Phnom Penh. Their hearts were still with their Khmer brothers and sisters who did not have the "luxury" of evacuation. They glued themselves to CNN news reports, scrutinized the *Bangkok Post* and listened eagerly to accounts of people coming out of Cambodia.

Some days the news was good, inspiring a confidence that the evacuated missionaries would soon be able to return to their homes and ministries. Other days the news was not promising, stirring up deep questions and concerns.

The group took advantage of some of Bangkok's facilities which provided an enjoyable distraction. Mike Roark found an outlet for his tension by jumping at the guest house director's request that he do some maintenance work. He spent ten days making plumbing and electrical repairs, trying to fix everything in sight.

The Cambodia missionaries were glad to hear from their colleagues on home assignment in the U.S. It encouraged their hearts to be told of their friends' prayers and of them gathering prayer support for the team from all around the U.S. They were not alone in this crisis.

Every morning for two weeks the team gathered after breakfast to read the Scriptures, pray together and rehearse their stories. One of the Bangkok missionaries met with the children and encouraged them to share their experiences and fears.

The bond between the members of the team was strengthened as each opened up his or her heart, often with deep emotion. There were those who longed to go back and those who, at times, didn't care if they ever saw Cambodia again. There were times of praise as the group recounted how God had protected them and flooded them with peace, often through His Word.

With great sorrow, they cried out to God on behalf of the people of Cambodia. Their thoughts turned to the ill and wounded who were unable to get medical attention, to those who had lost their homes, to the national pastors ministering in areas where fighting had been heavy. The waiting was the hardest.

A few days after arriving in Bangkok, David Strong read one morning from Lamentations 5:21, "Restore us to yourself, O LORD, that we may return. . . ." He recalled the morning the team had met and decided to leave Phnom Penh. That day he read from Psalm 80:19, "Restore us, O LORD God Almighty . . . that we may be saved." God had saved them from the war and He was restoring them as they waited and rested in Bangkok. From that day on, David believed that God would also grant the "return" in His time.

As the days passed, news coming out of Cambodia brightened. Soldiers of communist leader Hun Sen had successfully ousted co-prime minister Prince Ranariddh and had taken firm control of much of the country. The good news was that the prospect of civil war sounded less likely. Looting had diminished and security had apparently improved. The bad news was the unwelcome fact that a communist leader had taken control. What would that mean for the future of the Church? Would it be safe for the missionaries to return? Would they be allowed to return?

They decided that those questions could best be answered if some of them could see first-hand what was going on. So, on July 21, Don Weidemann, Steve Westergren and Bounoeuy Kes boarded a dual-propeller, sixty-passenger Royal Air Cambodge plane bound for Phnom Penh.

Pochentong International Airport was in better shape than they had expected. A freshly repaired section of the terminal took them through to the immigration check. Several bullet-damaged windows had yet to be replaced. And they saw areas where looting had taken place—even the lights and wiring had been removed.

The missionaries were met by a delegation of CAMA Services staff who were excited to see them. As they drove toward Tuol Koak, they could see evidence of the city's effort to get back on its feet. In some areas, people were at work cleaning up their buildings and hauling away debris. Other places still lay in ruins—gas stations which had been looted and torched, and car showrooms emptied of all but broken glass. Many stores remained closed.

They spent part of the afternoon visiting with the office staff, finding out how they were coping. And then they drove to the missionary residences around Tuol Koak. They knew the chances were good that their homes and vehicles would have suffered looting and theft. But to their relief, all were fine. Everything was exactly as it had been left.

Things were quiet in the neighborhood that

night—too quiet. The city was definitely not back to normal.

The next day they looked after banking and other business and then paid a visit to three government offices—the Ministry of Foreign Affairs, the Ministry of Religion and the Ministry of Health. At all three they received assurances that foreigners were wanted back, that missionary visas would be renewed, that things were much improved and that the future looked bright.

"If things are so good," Don wondered out loud, "then why are the Thai and Malaysian airlines still not flying? And why are the schools still closed?" There didn't seem to be any good answers.

Yet there was reason for optimism. A group of Cambodian pastors had come to the city for a meeting. In spite of the crisis, they were planning and praying for the future.

"It is a good thing you left the country," Yung Sot, the president of the national Church, told them. "There is still some antiforeign sentiment and the situation is not totally calm. There could still be fighting. Many people are not happy to see Hun Sen's troops living like kings with all that they looted from homes and stores. Reprisals may come."

Don, Steve and Bounoeuy returned to Bangkok on July 23 with cautious optimism for the future of Alliance missions in Cambodia.

"If the situation doesn't get any worse," they reported, "we can probably go back."

After two weeks in Bangkok, the team gratefully accepted an invitation to hold their annual field forum at Dalat School (the Alliance school for missionaries' children) in Penang, Malaysia. The forum had already been scheduled for the end of July in Cambodia. But since the door was closed there, they were happy to go to Dalat.

A twenty-two-hour train ride took them from the congested city of Bangkok to the relaxing seaside campus of Dalat with its manicured lawns and waving palm trees. Dr. Paul Bubna, president of The Christian and Missionary Alliance in the U.S., met them there.

The week allowed for times of rest and recreation, including long walks along white sandy beaches. Cool breezes and ebbing tides lapping lazily at the shore brought tranquility to questioning hearts. Each one had his or her own struggles to work through. For some it was a matter of being willing to return to the volatility of a nation teetering on the edge of civil war. For others it was being willing *not* to go back if that was how God directed.

Discussion at the business sessions revolved around "if " the team returned to Cambodia: How could they best minister to needy people *if* they went back?

The highlight of the forum was Dr. Bubna's encouragement and admonition from God's

Word. His messages on "choosing joy" from the book of Philippians were especially relevant in light of the less-than-joyful experiences of the previous few weeks.

He also spoke one night on the prophet Elisha. Doris Strong listened attentively to the message from Second Kings 6. Dr. Bubna pointed out that Elisha was a man of prayer and thus he "saw the invisible, believed the incredible and did the impossible."

Doris scratched those words into her notebook.

"Elisha lived in a world where God was sovereign," Dr. Bubna continued.

Doris' thoughts were racing. She knew that God was stretching her faith. It was one thing to recognize His hand in bringing them safely out of Cambodia and to give Him the praise for it. But it was quite another to recognize His sovereignty and trust Him enough to go back.

By the time Dr. Bubna reached the end of his message, Doris was enveloped in peace and knew that they were going back. The words of the closing hymn, "Lead On, O King Eternal," confirmed it.

Lead on, O King eternal,
    The day of march has come;
Henceforth in fields of conquest
    Thy tents shall be our home.
Through days of preparation
    Thy grace has made us strong,

> And now, O King eternal,
>   We lift our battle song.[1]

Doris wasn't the only one who had reached that conclusion. Others, sharing her peace and optimism, spoke of a renewed call to serve God and the people of Cambodia. The discussion had changed from "*if* we go back" to "*when* we go back."

The team met together to discuss their plans. There was no debate. There was no vote—just a unanimous decision that it was time to return to their homes and ministries in their adopted country.

*   *   *

By August 11, 1997, the entire team was back in Cambodia. They returned to find their homes untouched by thieves or vandals—everything was just as they had left it. The city was crawling out from under mounds of rubble created by the strife and was beginning to rebuild. Small houses were already sprouting up in areas that had been entirely routed by fire storms. Windows had been replaced, holes had been repaired, shops were open for business. The whole city seemed more peaceful than it had for months.

The worst of the fighting had taken place that first weekend in July, with the Phnom Penh missionaries in the midst of it. The feared

civil war did not become reality. And Battambang was spared the fighting that took place in
the capital. With the exception of the two
rocket-propelled grenades that exploded the
morning David Manfred and Bounoeuy Kes
left town, there was no fighting in Battambang.
So why did God direct the missionaries to
leave the country?

The five weeks they spent between Thailand
and Malaysia was not time wasted. God
worked in each of their hearts, teaching them
valuable lessons about trusting Him, no matter
what the cost. And He also worked in them as
a team: by sharing their prayers, griefs, struggles, vision and fears, the bond between them
was strengthened like never before.

Back in Cambodia, they were met with encouraging news. Jesus' promise to build His
Church was being fulfilled (see Matthew
16:18). Alliance congregations throughout the
country continued to meet in the missionaries'
absence. And the national leaders had decided
to set aside the last Saturday of each month for
prayer and fasting.

God used the time of fighting and insecurity
to strengthen and encourage Cambodian believers. Many of them related stories of oppor-
tunities they had to share the gospel. "All of
the foreigners have left," their neighbors
pointed out. "Why do you keep on believing in
a foreign God?" That question paved the way
for them to explain that their faith was not de-

pendent on foreigners, but on the true and living God.

The missionaries and church leaders were excited to witness a great responsiveness to the gospel. With once-suppressed memories of a brutal past resurfacing, in addition to a fear of the new communist government, people searched for peace. These circumstances, coupled with an increased volume of worldwide prayer being raised for Cambodia, prepared scores of hearts to understand and receive the good news of salvation through Jesus Christ.

The coup of 1997 does not stand alone on the pages of Cambodian history. It wasn't the first crisis the Alliance has faced on its soil, nor is it likely to be the last. Decades of turbulence have plagued the Cambodia road—a road rutted with pain, lined with heartbreak and watered with tears. The cost is high, but the rewards are greater. God is building His Church.

Endnote

[1] Ernest W. Shurtleff, "Lead On, O King Eternal," *Hymns of the Christian Life* (Camp Hill, PA: Christian Publications, 1978), #451.

Books by Lisa M. Rohrick

Any Road, Any Cost

In the Jaffray Collection of Missionary Portraits:

Both Feet on God's Path: The Story of Julie Fehr

In the Junior Jaffray Collection of Missionary Stories:

Beyond the Mist
Both Feet on God's Path
The Pearl and the Dragon
Tears for the Smaller Dragon